# News, Truth and Crime
## The Westray Disaster and its Aftermath

John L. McMullan

**Fernwood Publishing • Halifax**

Editing: Eileen Young
Cover photo: Kent Martin
Printed and bound in Canada by: Hignell Printing Limited

A publication of:
Fernwood Publishing
Site 2A, Box 5, 32 Oceanvista Lane
Black Point, Nova Scotia, B0J 1B0
and 324 Clare Avenue
Winnipeg, Manitoba, R3L 1S3
www.fernwoodbooks.ca


Fernwood Publishing Company Limited gratefully acknowledges
the financial support of the Department of Canadian Heritage,
the Nova Scotia Department of Tourism and Culture
and the Canada Council for the Arts for our publishing program.

Library and Archives Canada Cataloguing in Publication

McMullan, John L., 1948-
News, truth and crime : the Westray disaster and its aftermath /
John L. McMullan.

(Basics from Fernwood Publishing)
ISBN 1-55266-173-3

1. Westray Mine Disaster, Plymouth, Pictou, N.S., 1992--Press coverage.
2. Crime in mass media. 3. Corporations--Corrupt practices--Press coverage--
Case studies. 4. Disasters--Press coverage--Case studies. 5. Journalism--Objectivity.
I. Title. II. Series.

TN806.C22N6 2005    070.4'49363119622334'09716    C2005-904283-4

# Contents

*For*
*Deborah and Ashaya*

*I would say that this has always been my problem... the effects of power and the production of "truth"... my problem is the politics of truth.*
— Michel Foucault

*To understand cultural denial, we must first know what the media beast takes in, processes and then represents. This is a subtle operation, precisely because the media filter is so similar to cultural denial itself.*
— Stanley Cohen

*The pro-corporate tilt is nowhere clearer than in the way the press defines crime. Overwhelmingly, it is in terms of the personally inflicted violent offences... this definition has been ludicrously inadequate.... Yet the press constantly downplays serious corporate misconduct.... In newsrooms, the pro-corporate tilt is more often sensed than seen. It may be conveyed by editors at a daily news conference by silence, or it may take the form of self-censorship.*
—Morton Mintz

# Acknowledgements

Among the many people who have helped me write this book, some of whom have commented on it as a manuscript in part or in whole, I should like to express my thanks to the following: Gregory Barak, Steve Bittle, Lisa Kowalchuk, Chris McCormick, David Perrier and Paul Rock. I am also especially grateful to Stella Chiasson, Melissa McClung and David MacDonald for research assistance in collecting, coding and tabulating the data. They discussed and commented on aspects of the book as it was written. Melissa McClung, wrote her M.A. thesis on the press coverage of the public inquiry and was a particularly prescient assistant. I am grateful for her insights and reflective opinions.

This book is a "first move" in what I anticipate will be a systematic study of the Westray disaster and its aftermath. I am especially grateful to the Social Sciences and Humanities Research Council of Canada for their financial support and to Saint Mary's University for providing me with a course release. The former allowed the research to go ahead and the latter enabled the writing to proceed expeditiously. Without their assistance this book would not have been completed.

My partner, Deborah Findlay, has been a wonderful supporter of this project. Despite severe chronic fatigue illness, she never ceased to provide encouragement, love and understanding when it was most needed. Her critical review of the manuscript added enormously to the final product and I am grateful for her labour of love.

Ashaya, our dog, was a constant companion while this book was being written. She reminded me that going for walks and chasing sticks was just as important as writing words, no matter what I thought.

Lindia Smith prepared the final draft of this manuscript. She tolerated my many rewrites with patience, amusement and a generosity of spirit that other mortals could only wonder at in amazement. As is evident in the production of this manuscript, I benefited greatly from her technical skills.

Thanks also goes to Kent Martin, producer of the NFB film, *Westray* for use of the photo on the front cover.

I presented some of the materials included in this book in lectures, conferences and seminars at universities in Canada, the United States and Europe. I am grateful for these invitations and opportunities, and am indebted to those who took part in discussions on those occasions.

Errol Sharpe, the publisher at Fernwood, has been encouraging me to write a second edition of *Beyond the Limits of the Law: Corporate Crime and Law and Order* for some time now. Somehow I never seem to have gotten around to it. I hope that this small book, which is also about the topic of corporate crime, makes up for my delinquent behaviour. Once again, Errol has believed that my research should be published and circulated to an academic audience. Once again, I am grateful to him! My thanks also to Eileen Young and Beverley Rach for editorial and production assistance.

# 1. Introduction

On May 9th each year, the families and friends of the twenty-six men killed at the Westray Mine gather at Their Lights Shall Always Shine Memorial Park in New Glasgow, Nova Scotia to remember the dreadful morning when a mine exploded and resulted in death. This day remains a symbolic signifier of loss: a time and place where the deeply private becomes public again. This annual remembrance brings together not only the bereaved, and the lucky "survivors" who were off shift that day, but also the print and broadcast media, who report the remembering to regional and national audiences.

Westray is an event etched in popular memory in Atlantic Canada. Films, stage dramas, museum exhibits, radio shows, documentaries and fictionalized accounts have memorialized it. Amongst the public the word itself connotes a range of emotions: sorrow, anger and shame are arguably the most common. For many it is incredible that the investigations — regulatory, police, medical and criminal, as well as the public inquiry — produced no criminal convictions or convictions for breaches of mining and safety laws. To make matters worse, efforts to secure civil redress have recently failed. The government of Nova Scotia has steadfastly refused to accept responsibility for its part in the deaths at Westray; in the courts it has opposed providing financial compensation to the bereaved families. Wives, parents, children, brothers and sisters of deceased miners have coped with the legacy of Westray as best as they could. Some have struggled for justice, some have written about it, some have remembered death through annual commemorations and some have tried to forget and move on (Davis 2003).

From the very beginning Westray was a news event: the press have reported on it for over a decade. Like everyone else in this part of the world, I was an avid viewer and reader in the days and weeks after the explosion. Although I am no expert on mining disasters, I started to develop a sense of dread about the way in which the media selected, presented and constructed the representational reality of the Westray explosion. I was disappointed with the absence of investigative reporting and suspicious of the stories about "accidents," "mother nature" and the "inevitability of disaster" that characterized news making in the immediate aftermath of the explosion. Observing the media as they recorded and eavesdropped on private matters in the name of a human interest story, I was very disturbed by their disregard for the bereaved families. Equally troubling were corporate and state speculation, recounted by the press as "truths," about the explosion. News narratives too often framed the disaster as something surprising rather than socially predictable. Indeed the "truth" of Westray remains a highly contested matter. The bereaved, miners and their friends remain convinced that answers to the questions, "What happened?" and "Who is responsible?" have largely been ignored or dismissed (Dodd 1999). Fully 85 percent of fifty-two relatives recently interviewed felt that someone was still to blame for the loss of life; 58 percent still felt that justice had not been done (Davis 2003: 6).

From the outset, I thought that Westray was going to be a controversial matter of public interest. I suspected that the quickly appointed Richards Inquiry, and the RCMP investigation would be battlegrounds for vested interests. I expected that the medical examinations into the deaths would be painful and frustrating for the bereaved. I anticipated that the criminal trial would be an exhausting and disappointing encounter with a legal process that would probably be unable to address matters of liability involving accusations against powerful corporate and state offenders. I thought this way because I had spent the previous decade researching corporate crime and the failures of criminal justice systems to valorize the rights of those victimized by corporate and state harms and homicides.

I started to develop a "working file" on Westray within weeks of the explosion. Over the years, I have studied and compared thousands of newspaper accounts, court transcript pages and public inquiry documents. I have learned what experts, police, lawyers, judges, journalists, medical examiners, miners and bereaved family members have stated and restated about the explosion. I hope to write more about the "truth telling" experiences of the criminal justice process and the public inquiry in the near future. For now my focus is on the media, the politics of truth and the problem of corporate crime.

In September 1996, Sherman Hinze [an honours student] and I embarked on an initial study of the news coverage of the Westray explosion. This project culminated in 1999 with the publication of an essay entitled "The Press, Ideology and Corporate Crime" which was included in an anthology called *The Westray Chronicles: A Case Study of Corporate Crime*, edited by Chris McCormick (1999). I continued to do research on this topic; in 2001, I completed a second essay, "Westray and After: Power, Truth and News Reporting of the Westray Mine Disaster," which was published in a book entitled *Abusing Power: The Canadian Experience*, edited by Susan Boyd, Dorothy Chunn and Bob Menzies (2001). Both of these essays provided indepth investigations into the news representation of Westray as well as critiques of the role and excesses of the media in the reporting years between 1992 and 1995.

After the publication of "Westray and After," I obtained funding from the Social Sciences and Humanities Research Council of Canada to research and publish on all aspects of the disaster's aftermath from 1992 to 2002. The focus of this general project was to study the connections between power, knowledge and the production of truth in three related institutional sites: the media, the criminal justice system and the public inquiry, as well as among the bereaved families. In May 2002, I put together a research team of four — three graduate students (Stella Chiasson, Melissa McClung, David MacDonald) and myself — to study the media and Westray. Throughout 2002–2003 we collected, coded and tabulated over 2600 news reports on the explosion. Melissa McClung and I presented an initial paper, "Crime-Out: Press Reporting, News-Truth and the Westray Public Inquiry," at the Crime and Media Conference in Fredericton, New Brunswick, in October 2003 and a revised essay at the Canadian Studies Conference in St. Catharines, Ontario, in November of the same year.

This small book is the culmination of two years of work and completes the first phase of the research project. It is an exhaustive and an in-depth study of ten and a half years of news coverage. It is an analysis of how the press registered and re-registered truth about the explosion and the social reaction to it. In one sense, this research claims a fit with my earlier news studies and with the work of McCormick (1995), Richards (1999) and Goff (2001), who analyzed media coverage and the construction of Westray from 1992 to 1995. I have benefited greatly from their insightful works: where appropriate, I have compared and contrasted my findings with their results. However, this book claims a break with earlier research because it widens the research agenda to include shifting media discourses, and struggles about the production of truth, over a longer period of time. Media messages were hegemonic and subversive, and this book is both a confirmation of the organic process by which corporate and state voices try to generalize themselves as forms of cultural expression, and an exploration of the challenges to that power/truth regime. It is simultaneously a study of what was said, by whom, when, how and for what reasons, and a study of the silences contained in those narrative transactions. It is, above all, a study of the social organization of news discourses: the context of elicitation, the rules of elucidation, relevance and believability, and the strategic deployment of the telling of news narratives (Ewick and Silbey 1995: 206–209).

This book also claims to add to the growing field of media studies and corporate crime. In this body of literature, the media are criticized for missing, burying or covering up corporate crime news stories; reluctantly using the term "crime" to describe corporate harms and homicides; attaching blame to spurious causes such as "mother nature"; individualizing the representations of corporate crime via prominent personalities; "abnormalizing" corporate offending and obscuring its routineness; minimizing attention to causes of events in favour of attention to consequences; and inadequately understanding the organizational nature of corporate crime (Morash and Hale 1987; Mintz 1991; Wright, Cullen and Blankenship 1995; Lofquist 1999; Slapper and Tombs 1997; Lynch, Stretesky and Hammond 2000). Many of these media-based studies have the virtue of being focused in place and time, but the "media frames" are short-term — a matter of a few months or years of coverage. Frame developments and transformations over time are not typically examined, and the movement between contested and uncontested realms of news discourse are not usually captured or studied. With this present research, we can better examine the dynamic processes by which the press created an unfolding narrative about an event for over a decade. We can study how the press brought order to chaotic events by registering them as something that could be talked about again and again. We can explore the degree to which the news was a "site of struggle" on which various social groups contested claims about the causes, conditions and consequences of the Westray disaster.

I realize, of course, that "news" is one site in the media-crime-law relationship and not in any sense the only site. As Brown (2003: 31) rightly observes, the whole question of representation needs to be conceived "within a discourse of 'mediatization' which includes television, films, videos, novels, music, and the internet." But news itself may be approached as a cultural text in a broad-ranging sense as well. It is reasonable to purposefully delimit a field of study, recognizing, of course, that news is often framed in terms of dramatic narratives about heroes, fools and villains; these narratives make us cry, laugh and rage. Wykes writes sensibly in her introduction to *News, Crime and Culture* (2001: 1):

> Crime news... is the site of... national conscience and moral codes.... The continuum of criminality is... mediated through the news, which informs our view of the world, of others and of ourselves.

In giving thought to the media and the representation of Westray, I am indebted to several scholars. Michel Foucault's enduring contributions to the study of power, knowledge and discourse were inspirational. They provided me with a tool box of concepts, methods and ideas to see how the exercise of power produced "regimes of truth" about Westray and the conditions for the disqualifications of these "truth games." Hannah Arendt's work on the politics of lying and the practices of mendacity was significant, as was Stanley Cohen's recent work on states of denial. Both emphasized the importance of studying news talk as a way to uncover the accounts and rhetorical devices of the powerful and the press in the news-making process, including discourses of official denial and their changing narrative styles and structures. Howard Becker's ideas on a hierarchy of credibility were equally important as they reminded me that the moral right to be believed was unequally distributed and subjected to the plays of power, neutralization and normalization. Finally, Philip Scraton's work on the Hillsborough soccer tragedy in the United Kingdom served as an exemplar for this book. His insightful analysis of the media warned me that truth is a small word but a daunting concept. Establishing truth in regard to a disaster often means exposing the "degradation of truth" and then its "subsequent reclamation" (1999:11).

In that spirit, I think of this study as both an exercise in truthfulness and an exposé of the politics of truth and its absence. I realize that I am on difficult grounds here for there are those who would do away with the concept of truth altogether: stop pretending that truth can be the object of social inquiry and accept that it cannot be known is their postmodern counsel! But I am skeptical of their skepticism, which claims that there are no secure stateable truths. Indeed, if there is no truth, how does one explain the passionate pursuit of truthfulness? What are we supposedly being true to when we pursue truthfulness in the social sciences? As Carlen (2004: 260) wisely observes, "If no knowledge has any referential truth outside the discourses in which it is known, why ever bother to construct, deconstruct and reconstruct official discourse?" I have approached this study from the assumption that truth and truthfulness can be intellectually calibrated and stabilized in such a way that what we claim to be understandings about the truth of Westray and our chances of arriving at them can be shaped to fit with our need for truth telling and truthfulness. In this sense, my aim is to see how far the values of truth can be revalued, how news about Westray and its aftermath might be understood in a perspective quite different from that of its everyday, professional journalistic production. In attempting this I am mindful of the fact that official news discourse can play many roles, including supporting, subverting and repairing the status quo. Not unlike official inquiries, news as truth can nullify alternative truth accounts, or it can open up spaces of contestation between powerful official discourse and other accounts, allowing for reshaping and reconfiguration. What this points to is the need to take into account both the written and the unwritten, that which is made to appear and to disappear (Gilligan and Pratt 2004: 5).

In this book, I take up the question of power, discourse and the production of truth first, in Chapter Two. That chapter provides a conceptual introduction to my research problem and lays out my framework of analyses. Then, in Chapter Three, I provide a brief account of the explosion and the socio-legal reaction to it. My goal is to offer only a skeletal study of key socio-legal events so as to provide needed background for my main concern — the registration of news as a truth-telling exercise. Chapter Four discusses methodological issues around discourse analysis, sampling, coding of data content categories and news narratives. Chapter Five presents the findings of the research. It describes the prominence of Westray as news, the discursive connotations and their continuities, discontinuities and absences, and the relations between power, claims making and the production of news. Finally Chapter Six makes sense of the data, analyzes the significance of the findings for understanding the production of truth regimes and the invisibility of corporate crime, and compares and contrasts the news representation of Westray with other studies of the media and corporate crime.

# 2. Power, Discourse and the Production of News as Truth

## Introduction

It is important at the outset to consider the process of the production of truth and the exercise of power. Truth, Arendt (1971, 1972) reminds us, is a difficult concept. Its definition, identification and verification are rarely uncomplicated: they are almost always implicated in complex political and communicative processes involving perception, representation and interpretation. Yet civil proceedings, public courts, criminal investigations, special state tribunals, coroner's inquests, judicial reviews, public inquiries and truth commissions all claim, in theory at least, to offer mechanisms, rules and procedures by which "truth" can be aggregated, evaluated, and confirmed or denied. These agencies seek to elicit truth in people's stories, even if the narratives produced are usually restricted to formal recollections, which are then further refined by adversarial adjudication processes to narrower and narrower memories (Gilligan and Pratt 2004; Rothberg and Thompson 2000).

The evidence-bound character of these truth-seeking agencies, however, is not separate from the political context of the production of truth. The balancing of personal rights and freedoms, the questioning of political necessities and priorities, the entanglements of laws and the forgetfulness of sometimes disingenuous "official memories" together expose the myth of any simple or single truth and confirm that establishing "the facts" is not without controversy. Arendt (1971) distinguishes two forms of truth: "rational" truth, which posits the procedures and rules by which truth can be established, known and valorized, and "factual" truth, which is experiential and based on events that are observed, recorded and recollected. She notes that factual truth, which is the concern of this study, "is always in danger of being maneuvered out of the world," and it is infinitely more fragile than "axioms, discourses [and] theories" (231). The opposite of rational true statements is error, opinion or illusion; the opposite of factual true statements is the "plain lie." Indeed, mis-speaking the truth, she insists, has always been regarded as a necessary weapon in the arsenal of the powerful. But more recently these groups are organizing untruthfulness as a bulwark against the discovery of unsettling facts. This active aggressive capacity to manufacture disinformation is no longer about protecting state secrets, confusing hostile enemies or even deceiving others without deceiving oneself. Rather, as Arendt (1972) notes, it is increasingly about manipulating information about things that are not hidden at all; on the contrary, they are known to practically everybody, but are exempted from public discourse. In Cohen's (1993: 104) words, the idea is "to hide a presence from awareness"; this is not a matter of "lack of access to information, but an unwillingness to confront anomalous or disturbing information." This obfuscation of information is not only evident in the numerous rewritings of history denying atrocities to survivors, it is equally apparent in government programs, pronouncements and publications, in which, time and time again, known and established facts are ignored, decried, suppressed or rearranged if they hurt a powerful interest or subvert the credibility of a state agency (Cohen 2001).

Contemporary organized manipulations of the truth, then, do not so much tear a hole in the fabric of factuality as reconfigure the entire factual texture of society. Criminal justice institutions and religious institutions, for example, are just as capable of demonizing their clients, of denying their truths of injury and harm and of corrupting social justice as they are capable of acknowledging, adjudicating and resolving unsettling issues and troubling acts. Scraton, Jemphrey and Coleman (1995), in their study of the Hillsborough soccer stadium disaster in which ninety-six men, women and children died, remind us that the constitution, reconstitution and registration of truth often operated to protect police interests and their accounts of events while simultaneously denying justice to the victims through the dismissal of their voices. The recent revelations of "crimes of the clergy" tell us that for decades church authorities concealed awful facts about sexual abuse at the expense of their own faithful practitioners. They lied, ignored, misled and covered up truth to protect their own individual and institutional interests (Harris 1990; Berry 1992; Scheper-Hughes 1998). Nor does the press systematically cover all forms of crime. The distance between perception and reality is especially great in cases of crimes of the powerful, where those who report events are often as much concerned about how the story will be evaluated by others as they are with what "really" happened. The press can cover up as well as uncover; crime news discourse can explain away more than it explains (Mintz 1991). As Barak (1994: 34) notes:

> Lost in all of the crime and justice media hype… are the far more serious institutional exploits of the crimes of the powerful. Barely represented, let alone misrepresented, in the news in the late eighties and early nineties were such activities as the SandL thefts, the involvement of the BCCI in drug-money laundering and George Bush's millions in agriculture credits to Saddam Hussein via Banca Nationale del Lavaro… serious analysis of these crimes did not precede or follow these news presentations.

## The Press as a Site of Truth Telling

The press functions as an important site for the production and dissemination of "truth." Much of what we know about disasters, mass suffering and public atrocities, we know through mediated knowledge. As Barak astutely notes, the mass media "tend to reproduce a homogenization and recycling of images, texts and narratives that shape and influence our collective dreams and nightmares" (2003: 7). Codes of ethics claim that news should be accurate and factual; it should also be gathered with delicacy and circumspection. Journalists, we are told, should be mindful of privacy issues: they should show empathy in reporting cases involving grief, shock or sudden death. Of course, research on media coverage of disasters and atrocities reveals that the press can behave quite differently. They can exploit grief shamelessly, stigmatize people wrongfully, report awful rumor as fact and neglect unwelcome information. Icons of suffering tend to be represented in a graphic, personal and dramatic form (Barak 1994; Cohen 2001; Ericson et al. 1989; Fleras and Lock Kunz 2001; Moeller 1999; Potter and Kappeller 1998; Scraton et al. 1995; Surrette 1998). The Hillsborough disaster is again illustrative. The press decontextualized and depoliticized the event. Their reporting registered the truth as "soccer hooliganism" lubricated by excessive alcohol consumption. Blame and responsibility were placed on victims and bereaved family members when, in fact, negligent police decisions and actions about crowd control caused the tragedy and contributed to an aftermath of trauma where police interests denied truth and justice to the victims and survivors by concealing the facts from them (Scraton 1999; Scraton, Jemphrey and Coleman 1995).

The transition from lived experience to news narrative, however, does not occur in isolation. Gans (1980:80) defined news rather usefully as "information which is transmitted from sources to audiences, with journalists — who are both employees of bureaucratic commercial organizations and members of a profession — summarizing, refining, and altering what becomes available to them from sources in order to make this information suitable for their audiences." What constitutes news for the general public is usually transmitted via routine electronic or print-based media systems. This process of information acquisition, filtering, representation, interpretation and dissemination is not neutral, indifferent or unbiased. News-as-truth is highly selective and profoundly patterned. As Cohen (2001: 169) puts it, "the media do not tell us what to think, but they do tell us what to think about." Indeed the special genius of the news-making system is that it makes the "whole process seem so normal and natural that the very art of social constructionism is invisible" (Gamson et al. 1992: 174).

The mediation of news depends upon a number of distinct but inter-related factors that are extrinsic to an event's seriousness: geopolitical interests, market needs, advertising policies, organizational budgets, access to and control of information sources, cultural priorities and newsworthiness, and dominant discourses which enable, guide and sustain news coverage. On the one side are investments, markets, conglomerates and monopolies; on the other side are lobby groups, political agendas and the power to censure (Barak 1994; Adorno 1991; Fishman 1980; Hall et al. 1978; Rock 1973; Sumner and Sandberg 1990; Herman and Chomsky 1989). Global media ownership, markets and advertising interests and formats foster a "cheerleading" climate where pressures to turn a profit downplay images critical of corporations and simultaneously promote a corporate voice that is generalized across a broad range of cultural expression. Consumerism and commercialism combine to produce and distribute media images about corporations that are politically safe and economically enhancing.

While the media are often viewed as independent and determined in the pursuit of a "story" regardless of vested interests, news making is also guided by internal power mechanisms: editorial politics, story screening, the rhythms of the newsroom, the subculture of journalism and cognitive conceptions of "audience interest" are all designed to keep reporters and their texts within established ideological limits. News content is programmed so as to avoid upstaging advertising moods and biting the hands of global media empires, who own and run ever larger portfolios of newspapers, magazines, television stations, publishing houses and film studios. Reporters are urged to rely on official sources and routine channels, and as Gans (1980) suggests, this profoundly loads the news in favour of powerful corporate, political, military and scientific interests. Bourgeois culture restricts access to strategic information about business activities but allows corporations enormous control over the flow of images they convey and normalize to the public (Schiller 1986: 22). For example, reporters typically overestimate the criminality of those most vulnerable to authoritative labelling and sanctioning (Chibnall 1977; Ericson et al. 1989, 1991; Murdock 1982) and underestimate the harms and crimes caused by the powerful (Burns and Orrick 2002; Croall 1992; Friedrichs 1996; McCormick 1995; McMullan 1992; Randall 1987; Randall, Lee-Sammons and Hagner 1988; Smith 1992; Snider 1993). As Evans and Lundman (1983: 159) put it, "newspapers protect corporate reputations by failing to provide frequent, prominent and criminally oriented coverage of common corporate crimes." Similarly violence is often depicted as interpersonal violence rather than institutional and structural violence. Rarely does mass mediation expose the violence in the boardrooms or executive suites. Interpersonal acts of violence and their readerly texts "have legs and are recycled ad nauseam" while institutional acts of violence, "though more newsworthy, have no legs and are quickly forgotten" (Barak 2003: 15). As McQuail (1992: 273) reminds us, this is because the mass media typically follow rather than lead elites in defining social issues and trends. They are often instruments, not instigators, of social change!

When business crime is reported, it tends to be concentrated in up-market newspapers or specialist pages, focused on financial/economic matters, and framed in ways that demarcate it from "real" crime (Calavitta and Pontell 1994; Tombs and Whyte 2001). Thus Lynch et al. (1989), in their study of the Bhopal disaster; Cavender and Mulcahy (1998), in their analysis of General Motors and unsafe auto products; Wright et al. (1995), in their research on the fire at Imperial Food Products; Molotch and Lester (1978), in their study of the Santa Barbara oil spill; Lynch et al. (2000), in their research on chemical crimes; Goff (2001), in his study of the Westray explosion; Lofquist (1997), in his examination of the Akzo mine collapse; and Levi (1987), in his work on long-term fraud, all concluded that the press minimized corporate liability by refusing to use the term "crime" to describe events and by attaching blame to spurious causes such as geographical climates or regulatory failures.

Contrarily, for human rights issues to become news, victims have to convince news providers that their social suffering is unique and that strong denials from official sources are false. A "hierarchy of credibility" — Becker's (1967) term for the unequal moral distribution of the right to be believed — determines whether corporate sources, government spokespeople, expert witnesses, lawyers, victims or bereaved family members are heard, acknowledged or silenced. Typically, concepts such as deviant, immoral or criminal are produced through definitional processes that then apply terms unequally to certain categories of people. So news labels depend on who commits the acts and who is victimized. Crimes conducted by corporations are almost always ascribed a civil meaning, but the same crimes committed by individuals are ordinarily allocated a criminal status (Becker 1967, 1963: 13). As Cohen (2001:121) observes,

> A neat matrix predicts that items more likely to be selected [as news] will... deal with negative matters (violence, crises, and disasters) [and] consist of dramatic, sensational events rather than historical and unfolding problems.... But... no matrix can accommodate the sheer mass of events, political contingency and the vagaries of fashion.

Notwithstanding the volume of potential stories, the diversity of media forms and the number of presentational styles, the press remains fairly conventional in their reporting and representation of the news (Gamson et al. 1992; Tunnel 1998; Reiner 2002). While news may be a competitive arena of conflicting perspectives, it is one which is structurally and culturally loaded. The rules for the production of statements emphasize "importance" (what the public must know), "immediacy" (the present), "interest" (audience support), "individuals" (personalities), "credibility" (authoritative sources), "stigma" (binary categories) and "recollection" (retelling stories) (Fleras and Lock Kunz 2001: 70). So, for all the tensions, negotiations and flexibility that occur in the production process, the news media are as much an agency of social control as the police, courts and public inquiries whose activities they report on (Ericson et al. 1991: 74). The press reproduces order in the process of representing it: at bottom the underlying structure of communicative relationships is about power — "that deep sense of priority and legitimacy which is assigned both authority and responsibility to certain public sources of news and interpretation" (Williams 1989: 117).

The "media beast," to borrow Cohen's phrase, is not only a voluble truth teller, it proclaims and confers legitimacy on truth. And truth, as Foucault (1980a: 132) reminds us, is an "ensemble of rules according to which the true and false are separated and specific effects of power attached to the 'truth.'" It is produced by "virtue of multiple forms of constraint" and is not outside power or lacking in it. Rather, it circulates and "induces regular effects of power." Power is something that is exercised rather than possessed; it is not attached to interests but is incorporated in numerous practices that themselves directly imply knowledge and truth. It is not possible for power "to be exercised without knowledge, it is impossible for knowledge not to engender power" (Foucault 1977: 51). Power may refuse or deny; it also induces and produces discursive realities. It is a "productive work which runs through the whole social body" (Foucault 1989: 132).

Similarly, there is no power relation without the correlative constitution of a field of truth, nor any truth that does not presuppose and at the same time constitute power relations. Foucault (1980: 93) observes that "we are subjected to the production of truth through power and... power never ceases its interrogation, its inquisition, its registration of truth; it institutionalizes, professionalizes and rewards its pursuit." Of course, like power, truth is a phenomenon that works from the bottom up as much as it does from the top down. Its production is multidirectional; truth is coextensive with the social body. Truth flows through the instruments, mechanisms, practices and rituals through which it is deployed. Like power it is not a constant, exhaustive or static force. Just as resistance constitutes a condition of the existence of power, so too there is a dynamic of truth whereby knowledge speaks the truth to power, exposing established practices of truth making and truth telling. As Foucault (2001: 151) notes, there are four questions about truth telling that are of vital importance: "who is able to tell the truth, about what, with what consequences, and with what relation to power."

There are, to be sure, brave examples of investigative reporters unmasking the corruption of the powerful and bearing witness to very unwelcome facts. But, as I have observed elsewhere, journalists and reporters cannot easily take a stand that subverts corporate or powerful political interests (McMullan and Hinze 1999; McMullan 2001). The press is radically embedded in the production of "official" discourses that form part of a society's "general politics of truth": the appropriate political technologies of truth discovery; the enunciations that a society deems acceptable or not; the mechanisms it uses to judge true and false statements; the sanctioning of statements; and the valorization of claim makers as truth sayers (Foucault 1980c: 137). This process of truth production often works through the symbolic rewarding and sanctioning (sometimes explicitly, sometimes implicitly) of good and bad acts. Symbolic rewarding identifies heroes, victims and neutral characters, and associates them with certain traits, beliefs or types of deeds. Symbolic punishment stigmatizes certain activities or traits as undesirable or deviant. But these constructions occur against the backdrop of embedded, taken-for-granted, normal social understandings and social arrangements (Barak 1994: 13).

Truth claims are anchored in discourses and discursive formations that produce particular ways of organizing thinking, talking and doing in regard to selected topics. The external world is mediated through language that, in turn, constitutes social subjects, the identities of persons and their social relations and habitus, but only within the context of institutional practices. Words matter because they are part of a wider framework of tactical and strategic intelligibility. Discourses enable sets of linked signs — speech, texts, physical acts and visual symbols — to form grids that structure experience, feeling, thought and action, and prevent other things from being said, felt or done. They are practices that systematically form the objects of which they speak. The questions posed by discourse are these: how is it that one particular statement appears rather than another, and how does that statement fit into a network that has its own condition of existence. While statements are the "molecular unit," they do cluster into "systematic unities." To quote Foucault (1988a: 38),

> whenever one can describe, between a number of statements, such a system of dispersion, whenever, between objects, types of statements, concepts or theocratic choices, one can define a regularity (an order, correlations, positions and functionings, transformations)… we are dealing with a discursive formation.

This means that discourses and discursive formations appear, correlate and redraw. They are both continuous and discontinuous. Because discourses govern the construction of objects — such as how criminality is an object of medical expertise, or how sexual deviance is an object of psychiatric discourse — they are potentially subversive. Those in power seek to exercise control over discourses that they consider threatening because they have "real effects" and produce the "conditions of possibility" of resistance and replacement. In Foucault's (1981: 52–53) words, "discourse is the power which is to be seized, because it authorizes the right to speak and be taken seriously or not."

For Foucault (1980a: 133), the authority of the press is not narrowly institutional, reducible to organizational structure or internal discursive dynamics; rather, it extends to the representation, registration and ordering of knowledge, linked in elective affinity with "systems of power which produce and sustain it, and to effects of power which it induces and which extend it." The press, like government, is a "meta-power" buttressed and sustained by "micro-power networks" that feed and energize "the capillaries of power." These webs of social alignment involve radio, cable and television stations, newspapers, magazines and internet sites, as well as their authoritative sources, who produce and circulate words, signs, symbols and images for mass consumption. What the media typically produce is a "regime of truth" or a "general apparatus of truth" that is anonymous, formalized and coherent in character (Foucault 1980a). "Regimes of truth" are discursive practices of immense intensity and contestation. They are not counterpoised to falsity or error; rather, "regimes of truth" lay down what is true and what is false through a "prodigious machinery" designed to restrict, downplay or forbid other competing truths (Foucault 1981). Embedded in discourse, they are marked by "rules of formation" that define "objects, operations, concepts and theoretical options," "limits and forms of the sayable" and "criteria of correlation" that situate discourses among others as well as among non-discursive institutions (Foucault 1991a, 1991b, 1988a, 1988b). In Foucault's (1991c) words, "practices don't exist without a certain regime of rationality" that produces "procedures" for examining, classifying and doing things, and "codes" for deciding principles and for justifying how they are accomplished.

"Apparatuses of truth" can be dominant or subordinate depending on relations of power and authority. Hierarchies of credibility certainly exist. On the one hand, holders of state institutional power and corporate power not only try to manage the labels of deviant and criminal (applying them to certain acts and not to others), they also construct and arrange the truth so that their versions of veracity gain credence over others. This occurs most visibly in their relations with the media. Corporations often deploy "experts," who cater to a journalist's need for quick news, by providing background briefings, press conferences, press releases, etc., while simultaneously shaping, making and manipulating a story (Awad 1985). Corporate sources filter narratives, images and explanations through media outlets, often transforming or neutralizing their violent and harmful deeds into seemingly "normal" business principles and practices. Corporations and governments invest in the symbolic politics of news advertising because "sophistication in defending bad news and trafficking in good news is seen as an essential part of achieving capital gains" (Ericson et al. 1991: 14). They exercise power through the production of truth that they interpolate, and the media, in turn, are constrained to a large degree to adhere to this alteration of the truth, thereby producing the truth of their power. On the other hand, discourses do not simply express or reproduce already constituted social relations. The exercise of power provokes exercises of resistance, and the status of truth is never absolutely determined. Discourses are sometimes unruly; they proliferate, compete and collide. They are continuous unities, but they are also dispersed practices that "cross each other, are sometimes juxtaposed with one another, but can just as well exclude as be aware of each other" (Foucault 1981a: 67). Discourses are strategic games of struggle, of confrontation, of control, of subjection, of qualification and of disqualification. As Rouse (1994: 112) notes, "to make truth-claims is to try to strengthen some epistemic alignments, and to challenge, undermine, or evade others." To criticize power is to participate in "counter-alignments to resist or evade its effects."

Truth then is not simply imposed on people. Rather, it is invested in them and exerts pressures on them, just as they themselves, in the struggle over truth, resist the grip it has on them (Kendall and Wickham 1999). The "power of truth" can be distanced from hegemonic sites and institutions within which it operates: a "new politics of truth" can be constructed (Foucault 1980a: 133). Dominant forms of knowledge do fall into disuse, while subjugated knowledges, whose validity is not dependant on the approval of established regimes of authority, can be registered and validated (Foucault 1980d: 82). By subjugated knowledges I mean buried or masked knowledges as well as unqualified or disqualified knowledges that are below the required level of expert erudition, but that appear or reappear from the margins to form "counter memories" or "genealogical fragments" of dissent (Foucault 2003: 7–9). So preferred readings of events can be subverted and contested meanings created that recast and reinterpret what Arendt calls "the factual truth" of corporate crime. As she (1971: 231) puts it, "facts and events… occur in the field of ever-changing affairs of men, in whose flux there is nothing more permanent than the admittedly relative permanence of the human mind's structure." Communicating media messages is to some degree "open": it involves "viewers' work," where the dominant theme invited by a news text may be reaffirmed, refused or re-negotiated. Indeed the more "thematic" and less "episodic" the news coverage, the more likely readers are to hold public officials accountable for causing social problems or for alleviating them (Iyengar 1991). News narratives are, in some instances and under certain circumstances, sites of struggle where the powerful are forced to compete and defend what they would prefer to have accepted for truth.

## Denial, Disputation and the Registration of Truth

In discussing media coverage of disasters such as Westray, it is important to recognize that the relationship between power and truth is organized in a highly specific fashion. "Truth" is often recorded through professional discourses that strategically "take charge" of social issues: this occurs in the fields of science, engineering, business, medicine and law, to name a few. These groups produce definitional concepts of credibility, establish a conventional genre of presentation, mobilize official discourses and induce effects of power through moral claims making (Becker 1963). In turn, their "disciplines" are often accredited as authoritative news sources about public health, war, crime, social disasters and the like. Not surprisingly, those in power are persistent in their efforts to construct and reconstitute their hegemony through technical investigations, scientific studies, medical advisories, criminal trials, public inquiries and media stories (Moeller 1999; Scraton et al. 1995; Tunnel 1998). In Foucault's (1991c: 81) words,

> we are dealing with sets of calculated, reasoned prescriptions in terms of which institutions are meant to be reorganized, spaces arranged, behaviors regulated.... These programs crystallize into institutions, they inform individual behavior, they act as grids for the perception and evaluation of things.

It is at the point at which institutional and professional discourses intersect that "views from above" become strategically organized and rationalized, while "views from below" become disputed and disqualified. Arendt (1971, 1972) and Cohen (1993, 1996, 2001) identify three forms of reaction that are part and parcel of official denial: "(a) literal denial or the politics of lying — 'nothing is happening'; (b) interpretive denial — 'what is happening is really something else'; and (c) implicatory denial — 'what is happening is justified.'" Literal denial involves corporate, government and media rearrangements of damaging information into less harmful narratives; blatant attacks on the reliability and credibility of critical storytelling; and the trivializations of moral claims and accounts "from below" (Cohen 2001: 105). Interpretive denial is the standard alternative to literal denial: "Admit the raw facts but deny the interpretive framework placed on the events" (Cohen 2001: 105). Interpretive denial attempts to cognitively redefine events and reallocate them to a different, less detracting order. This is a more complex form of denial: it entails claims and counterclaims that arise "because the dominant language of interpretation is legal" (Cohen 2001: 106). Because law is a "plastic medium of discourse," state, corporate and media interests frame and reframe, and name and rename events, through "games of truth" that apply euphemistic labels to harmful and deadly acts or that use the law to cloud facts with rhetorical devices and technical distinctions. Interpretive denial creates "an opaque moat between rhetoric and reality" (Cohen 2001: 108). Implicatory denial reinterprets wrongdoing and justifies it in a language of righteousness ("justice had to be swift"); necessity ("we had to do it"); self defence ("they deserved it"); context ("you can't see the whole picture"); and favourable comparison ("look what they did"). While these three forms of denial are often retrospective inventions approximating justifications or excuses, Cohen recognizes one other form of denial. "Passive denial," he says, pays no attention to the situation at all. It is an absence of response in which non-acknowledgement and non-engagement is the "most radical form of silence possible" (Cohen 2001: 103). It signals the absence of a problem to those whose interests it seeks to protect.

Taken together, these "vocabularies of denial" are primary manifestations of the exercise of power and the registration of the separation of the officially true from the false. There are, of course, ongoing battles over the rules for determining status of truth and the economic and political roles that it plays. As Gamson et al. (1992) observe, truth is not a monolith exclusively defined by the media in a hegemonic power formation. Official viewpoints do not always monopolize the news-making process. Rather, the press represents a site of struggle where powerful and less powerful interest groups compete, define and defend what should be taken for truth. As they put it, there is room "to offer competing constructions of reality" (Gamson et al. 1992: 373). Truth commissions, for example, have validated victims' experiences of suffering and provided spaces for subaltern perspectives to be heard, understood, memorialized and officially recognized (Leman-Langlois and Shearing 2004; Rothberg and Thompson 2000). Similarly, public inquiries have been deployed as official acknowledgers of wrongdoing and promoters of shared truths about disturbing conduct. They have disclosed anomalous acts and embarrassed and shamed their perpetrators (Gilligan 2004; Hancock and Liebling 2004; Tucker 1995).

Dominant power players do not have a monopoly in defining "truth" discourses. As Foucault (1980e: 100–101) notes, "discourses can be both an instrument and an effect of power, but also a hindrance, a stumbling block, a point of resistance and a starting point for an opposing strategy." Journalists can develop critical plot lines that resist dominant discourses. They can formulate stories of refusal that directly question the conventionality of authoritative wisdom. They can open up the status of truth by disrupting commonly held conceptions about events and social practices. Readers of the news can use media imagery innovatively and reverse intended messages. As Fiske (1987) observes, no text can control and unify all meanings embedded within it. Irony, humour, metaphor and hyperbole create collisions of discourses significant enough to prise open potential unintended meanings. But in their official discourses, especially around the rule of law and the production of news, the powerful have been especially adroit at avoiding blame, condemning others and decontextualizing people and events from the structural, material world of cause and consequence (Scraton 2004; Lea 2004). They have attempted to close down "open" meanings in favour of preferred ones by channelling the news spectacle to their ends. The press, for their part, are not necessarily biased toward the powerful but their cultural assumptions and bureaucratic structures predispose them to act as conduits of that power, no matter how much they announce their autonomy (Lofquist 1997; Scraton et al. 1995; Reiner 2002; Smith 1992). As Gamson et al. (1992) observe, the media "promote apathy, cynicism, and quiescence" and the trends are toward "more and more messages, from fewer and fewer producers, saying less and less." This does not mean, however, that there is no good news. The media can convey narrative contradictions that enable both order and change. Paletz and Entman (1981), for example, found that the press shifted its coverage of the Vietnam War over a ten-year period. They became more critical, although they framed opposition to the war as a responsible position only after the war had lost its legitimacy with both activists and elites. As Barak (1994: 16) puts it, the news media is multi-rather than one-dimensional encompassing the contradictory roles of lapdog on behalf of the powers that be, watchdog on behalf of the citizens that be, and neuterdog on behalf of the value-neutral journalists that be.

However, before examining the media and organized news telling, it is important to know how power was exercised in the aftermath of the Westray explosion. How did personal loss become public property? What was the socio-legal reaction to death underground? What were the families' experiences of Westray and after? How did the socio-legal context situate the press procedures for the production of Westray's truth?

# 3. The Explosion and the Aftermath

The Westray Explosion

At 5:20 a.m. on May 9, 1992, an explosion ripped through an under-ground mine in Plymouth, Pictou County, Nova Scotia, claiming the lives of twenty-six miners, eleven of whom remain buried underground to this day. According to the *Report of the Westray Mine Public Inquiry*, sparks caused by the cutting head of a continuous miner machine ignited meth-ane gas. This, in turn, caused a large rolling flame to develop, which travelled inside the mine, consuming all the oxygen in its path and leaving behind deadly carbon monoxide. The methane fire intensified into a methane explosion. The shock wave from the explosion then caused dust particles to become airborne; this created a full-blown coal-dust explosion underground (Richard 1997).

The explosion was so strong that it blew the top off the mine entrance, more than a mile above the blast centre. In the nearby villages, houses shook and windows broke. Residents were awakened from their beds; within minutes phones began to ring and people were put on alert to cope with what one woman described as "this incredible thud... a noise that filled the atmosphere.... Oh, my God! The vastness of this" (cited in Richards 1999: 144).

The explosion crushed the miners on the spot or poisoned them where they stood. In either event, death was almost certainly instantane-ous. Pictures from the mine site show a scene of utter destruction. Steel roof supports were shattered. Steel doors were blown apart. Equipment lay burned and twisted into piles on the ground. The mine walls were split and cracked wide open in places. The mine floor was littered with tons of fallen debris and brick. The air was deadly poisonous: draegermen and later police investigators had to use special breathing equipment to search for survivors and evidence. When the bodies were brought to the surface they were badly burned. Clothing was literally scorched off the skin. Some bodies had turned bright red, the result of carbon monoxide poisoning. All were marked by signs of intense heat. Hair was singed and hands were closed into tight fists (Richard 1997; Richards 1999: 144).

Disasters claim lives, disable and traumatize while ordinary people go about doing their ordinary business in private or in public, at work or at play. They are routinely caused "by a coincidence of predictable circum-stances coming together unexpectedly" (Scraton 1999: 83). Often, the first rescuers are survivors themselves; then come the emergency services — police, volunteers, medical officers, social workers, grief counsellors and the clergy. Essential to disaster management are agreed procedures to bring order from chaos: where to hold the dead; how to accommodate survivors, relatives and friends; who and how to identify the bodies; when and how to seal the site for investigation; and how to provide accurate information to an anxious public. Hospitals have to be put on alert; telephone "trees" have to be mobilized to bring in needed staff quickly; temporary mortuaries have to be designated, briefing rooms have to be set up; the media have to be "plugged-in"; and relations between distressed relatives, the press, the police and the employer have to be spatially arranged to manage communications, permit the expression of anxiety and grief and reduce potential conflicts between assembled parties.

In the early hours after the explosion, numerous groups positioned themselves to prepare for, respond to and understand the disaster. The families of the trapped miners and their friends gathered to provide support and await information. The media, local and international, converged on Plymouth to report the story. Curragh Resources, the owners of the Westray Mine, took control of the site, managed the incident and produced and dispersed information that became news. The company installed the families in a fire hall across from the mine; a community centre, directly opposite the fire hall, was turned into a media centre. The RCMP patrolled the road separating the two buildings, managed the flow of traffic and isolated the families from the media. Reporters and family members were kept away from company offices. The entire site had the feel of a siege: information was strategically gathered and released; trust and openness were in short supply (Richards 1999: 146–48).

Draegermen — miners trained in rescue operations — arrived on the scene and quickly went into action. They spent the next week picking their way through the debris, looking for survivors (Comish 1993). On Day Two, they discovered eleven bodies. On Day Five, they retrieved four more. The dead were taken to a nearby hockey arena which served as a temporary morgue. There they were identified and examined. But on May 14, Curragh Resources announced that there were no survivors and that the search underground was too dangerous to pursue any further. When the family members demanded a plan for retrieving the remaining eleven bodies, a Curragh Resources executive responded in an astonishingly callous manner: "We're here to make money, not spend money, and if you want to get your bodies back, go see your politicians" (Dodd 1999: 232). This deeply hurt and angered the bereaved as they soon realized they would never see or touch their loved ones again. Their sons, brothers, fathers and partners were no longer theirs to hold. To the company, the eleven dead were now simply their bodies, entombed in their mine. In the end, the provincial and federal governments sided with Curragh Resources, and the mine was flooded. The remaining bodies remained unclaimed, an unpopular decision in mining communities committed to recovering their dead for proper burial (Dodd 1999).

Within weeks of the explosion, the personal and social impacts of the tragedy had extended beyond those directly involved, affecting entire communities and professionals from outside the communities. Almost immediately, the Premier of the province promised a public inquiry and on May 15th, after rescue efforts were abandoned, he appointed Justice Richard, a judge of the Nova Scotia Supreme Court, to investigate the disaster. "Nothing and no person with any light to shed on this tragedy," the Premier insisted, "will escape the scrutiny of this inquiry" (Province of Nova Scotia 1992). The Department of Labour, which had had oversight responsibilities for the Westray mine since its inception in 1988, also launched an internal review and investigation into the causes of the explosion. The police, normally a pre-eminent group in post-disaster tragedies, were slow to develop an investigative role. Nevertheless, by May 21, twelve days after the explosion, the RCMP initiated their own criminal investigation. Three separate investigations were in process in the immediate aftermath of the explosion and a company-paid panel of experts had been hired to conduct an internal corporate assessment of the disaster. Inevitably, personal loss quickly became public property (McCormick 1995, 1999).

## The Regulatory Regime and Non-Compliance

Even though the public was shocked by the explosion, bereaved family members were not truly surprised. In nine months of operation, Curragh Resources had been cited for excessive levels of methane gas, poor ventilation underground and explosive levels of coal dust on the mine floor. In fact, inspectors had visited the mine over fifty times since 1988, and their reports revealed that mine managers were repeatedly warned to clean up the mine site in order to prevent an explosion (Glasbeek and Tucker 1999; Jobb 1999). On April 29th, ten days before the disaster, an inspector issued a written order threatening prosecution unless a coal dust prevention plan was implemented. But the mine blew up before the fourteen-day waiting period had elapsed (Richard 1997: 62).

The Department of Labour pursued a non-confrontational, compliance approach to overseeing the mine. This encouraged a culture of indifference between Curragh Resources and provincial inspectors, and a conflict of interest between local politicians who had lobbied for the Westray project and regulators who tried to monitor it (Richard 1997). The Premier, for example, convinced the federal government to invest $85 million to finance the mine, and his own government provided a $12 million loan, infra-structure incentives and a fifteen-year take-or-pay contract with the Nova Scotia Power Commission to supply 700,000 tons of coal per year at three times the market rate (Glasbeek and Tucker 1999, Tucker 1995). Profits were put ahead of people. Miners could not convince mine managers to prioritize safety over production. Several quit, while others who complained were intimidated. Those who went directly to labour department officials were told that their hands were tied. Still others who remained at Westray worked in fear, hoping beyond hope that they could defy injury or death. A "mock bureaucracy" prevailed at the mine site: managers, workers and inspectors were aware of rules, but they made few attempts to adhere to them because they held no legitimacy (Hynes and Prasad 1999).

It was not until October 1992, almost six months after the explosion, that Nova Scotia's Department of Labour finally filed fifty-two charges against Curragh Resources and two mine managers, alleging violations of the *Occupational Health and Safety Act* (Province of Nova Scotia 1996) and the *Coal Mines Regulation Act* (Province of Nova Scotia 1989). But their actions were too little, too late. They failed to censure Curragh Resources and its officials for their role in the explosion. By April 1993 the fifty-two charges were dropped in favour of a criminal prosecution. Based on the principle of double jeopardy, both sets of charges could not be advanced at the same time. So the violations under the regulatory statutes were abandoned without much thought as to the consequences (Jobb 1994; 1999).

## The Police and the Problem of Prosecution

The police were certainly on the scene within minutes of the explosion. But the RCMP were mostly concerned with monitoring a social crisis: media management, traffic control and body identification were their main activities. It was not until September 17th, four months after the explosion, that they secured the mine site and seized company records and equipment. Over the next several months they entered the mine site and collected evidence to support charges of criminal negligence and manslaughter against Curragh Resources and against two mine managers. They seized material evidence inside the mine including coal dust samples, methane monitoring devices, a miner's diary and mining machinery. Through on-site investigations and interviews with witnesses they learned that Curragh Resources had failed to properly train miners for underground work, that ventilation inside the mine was inadequate, that measures to reduce coal dust were not implemented and that methane detectors had been illegally altered to keep mining machines operating when methane levels were above the legal limit (Jobb 1994, 1999; McCormick 1999; Richard 1997).

From the very beginning, however, the criminal prosecution was ill-equipped to handle the highly technical, complicated Westray case. The Director of Public Prosecutions did not assign staff to the case full-time until September 1992. The RCMP had been investigating the causes of the explosion for months, but prosecutors were not present to provide timely advice about warrants, searches and appropriate investigative procedures. The two prosecutors assigned to the case were inexperienced and overworked. They expressed concerns that the government was not properly funding and resourcing the case against Curragh Resources and its officials. Assigned to working in a spare office with inadequate budgets, little expertise and no support staff, they eventually resigned in early 1993. Their last memo to the Director of Public Prosecution was prescient:

> We have been maintaining responsibility for the largest criminal prosecution in the history of the province without offices, desks, telephones or full-time support staff for the last five-and-one-half months.... If we cannot do the job properly, we cannot do it at all (cited in Jobb 1999: 174)

They claimed that the provincial government was too deeply implicated in the explosion to be relied on to effectively finance the criminal justice prosecution. Before the case went to trial, the prosecutors prophetically predicted it would fail to produce a just resolution for both the victims and the accused.

Meanwhile, the RCMP were placed in the precarious position of presenting a complicated and heavily documented criminal case without the legal guidance of the Crown lawyers (Jobb 1999, 1994; McCormick 1995; Tucker 1995). Not surprisingly this resulted in police errors. Under the *Criminal Code*, the police cannot seize evidence for more than three months without laying charges, unless, of course, they obtain a court order for a longer period. The RCMP failed to seek an extension on the warrant. Immediately, the defence attorneys demanded that this evidence be handed over to them for purposes of cross-examination. The judge resisted this legal request, but cautioned the prosecution to follow the letter of the law. He granted the police one more month to lay charges or lose evidence pertinent to the case. On April 20th, 1993, the RCMP laid charges of criminal negligence and manslaughter against the company and two mine managers. But, like the first team, the new prosecutors were not prepared to handle the highly technical case. As soon as the criminal charges were laid, they were contested. Provincial Court Judge Patrick Curran deemed them too vaguely worded to allow Curragh Resources and the mine managers a fair defence. The RCMP and Crown prosecutors redrafted the charges. They withstood a second challenge, but the case was already severely crippled. The criminal justice process, it seems, was stumbling before it could stand (Jobb 1994, 1999; McCormick 1995).

## The Criminal Trial and Its Aftermath

The Premier had early on promised a comprehensive public inquiry to explore the causes of the explosion, the political circumstances surrounding mine development and the role of health and safety inspectors in providing oversight. The public inquiry hearings were scheduled for late in 1992, but they were suddenly suspended. Could criminal proceedings exist concurrently with a public inquiry? Could the families' demands for accountability and justice be squared with the constitutional rights of Curragh Resources and its managers to a fair trial? Were the initial terms of reference of the inquiry so broad that they overlapped with those of the criminal law? Legal experts wrestled with these questions for some time, but defence lawyers for Curragh Resources and its managers had little difficulty convincing the provincial government to ban public inquiry hearings until the criminal prosecutions were completed. If made to testify at the inquiry, they argued, their clients would be denied their constitutional right to remain silent, and their testimony would be used against them in the criminal courts. In November 1992 the Nova Scotia Supreme Court struck down the public inquiry. Examining evidence to establish culpable neglect, they opined, was synonymous to establishing criminal negligence. This, the Nova Scotia Supreme Court insisted, was a criminal justice issue to be heard under federal, not provincial, jurisdiction. The provincial government was invited to redraft the terms of reference of the inquiry, but they declined; instead, they challenged this ruling in the Court of Appeal. In January 1993 the Court of Appeal overturned the Nova Scotia Supreme Court's decision to strike down the inquiry, and it was reinstated under its original terms of reference. But the inquiry hearings had to be delayed until the criminal trial was concluded. In effect, the public inquiry's future was in the shaky hands of the Crown prosecutors and the RCMP. It would not commence hearings until November 6th, 1995 (Jobb 1994; McCormick 1995).

After 1003 days of allegations, frustration, legal battles and political wrangling, the Westray trial commenced on February 6, 1995, with a new team of Crown prosecutors. Right from the beginning criminal wrongdoing was secondary to technical disputes over disclosure of Crown evidence. After hearing evidence from twenty-three witnesses, Justice Anderson suddenly halted the trial on March 2, 1995. He secretly contacted the Prosecution Service's Director and blamed the lead prosecutor for the disclosure problems that were slowing the trial proceedings. He demanded that the prosecutor be removed from the case. The Prosecution Service Director immediately revealed this incident to the Crown lawyers. They, in turn, criticized Justice Anderson for interfering in the criminal justice process and argued that his actions were biased against the Crown. They demanded a mistrial, but Justice Anderson refused. The Crown then secured an emergency hearing before the Supreme Court of Canada on April 5th. But this court ruled that it did not have jurisdiction to intervene in mid-trial. Ironically, they ordered Justice Anderson to evaluate the merit of his own actions. Not surprisingly, he deemed his actions appropriate and within jurisdictional bounds: he ordered the trial to proceed. Then, on June 9th, Justice Anderson stayed the criminal charges against Curragh Resources and its managers. He accepted a defence motion that the Crown's failure to disclose evidence amounted to an abuse of process. The Crown appealed to the Nova Scotia Court of Appeal and in December 1995 Anderson's decision was overturned. On appeal, the charges were reinstated and the Crown was not deemed responsible for non-disclosure. The Westray case, the Appeal Court argued, was unique. It involved extensive and highly technical documents, and the Crown could not be expected to disclose all of their evidence as promptly and efficiently as in other criminal cases. The Court of Appeal agreed with the Crown that Justice Anderson's actions were biased against them. They ordered a new trial with a different judge (Jobb 1999; McCormick 1999).

The prosecution service, headed by a new director and funded by a new government, tried again to prosecute the Westray case. But the defence appealed the decision for a retrial to the Supreme Court of Canada in an attempt to have the charges stayed once and for all. On March 2, 1997, the Supreme Court upheld the Appeal Court's decision. In a seven-to-two decision, it ruled that Justice Anderson's actions were biased against the Crown. Two dissenting judges, however, also condemned the Crown's handling of the case. They cited a litany of abuses: the Crown had misled the court, ignored court orders, broken rules of procedure, not disclosed evidence in a timely manner and attempted to cover up mistakes. In the end, all judges agreed that systemic failures had tainted the state's criminal case. They ordered the Crown to repay the legal costs incurred by the defendants (Beveridge and Duncan 2000; Jobb 1999).

Following this decision, however, the Crown did not return to court. Instead, the province's Director of Public Prosecution ordered internal reports to assess the Crown's case and the likelihood of conviction, and external reviews to evaluate the public prosecutors' role in assembling the Westray case, including their relationship with the government and their refusal to contribute sufficient resources to the case. In the end, the Prosecution Service was absolved of responsibility for the failures of the criminal prosecution. In July 1998, however, the Prosecution Service accomplished what the defence, the Court of Appeal and the Supreme Court of Canada was unable to do. They stayed the criminal charges against the Curragh Resources managers for good. Disagreements among mining experts about the cause and spread of the explosion, they argued, made a criminal conviction unlikely (Beveridge and Duncan 2000). After hearing forty-four days of testimony that produced sixty-seven hundred pages of court transcript and cost over three million dollars, no one was held criminally responsible for the deaths of twenty-six miners.

## The Public Inquiry

On May 4, 1995, the United Steelworkers of America, the union representing the Westray miners, initiated an appeal to the Supreme Court of

Canada that revived the public inquiry before the criminal prosecutions were completed. This decision was precipitated by the defendants' decision to be tried in a criminal court by judge alone. The earlier stated concern that publicity surrounding the inquiry would prejudice a jury was no longer compelling to the Supreme Court of Canada. It restored the public inquiry and made the government of Nova Scotia responsible for deciding whether an inquiry, a criminal justice prosecution, or both should proceed. By delaying an inquiry in favour of a criminal justice prosecution, one Supreme Court judge argued that the government risked losing its ability to establish truth and attribute blame and accountability for wrongdoing. According to this judge, the confidence crisis is especially poignant when a government and its agents are implicated in the harms committed and the remedies delayed or denied (Jobb 1999; McCormick 1999).

After five years of legal wrangling and judicial indecision, the long-anticipated public inquiry was allowed to proceed. Over the years, bereaved family members and miners had become skeptical about the government's ability to uncover and tell the truth about the Westray explosion and about its ability to promote social justice for victims and survivors (Dodd 1999; Davis 2003; McCormick 1999). This distrust was further exacerbated by the government's reluctance to disclose hundreds of documents that were withheld from the public under claims of confidentiality and cabinet secrecy. Six weeks before the inquiry hearings started, however, the government released most of the sequestered documents (cabinet discussions, legal opinions and financial records) to the public inquiry.

The inquiry began hearing testimony on November 6, 1995. Miners, mining experts, labour inspectors, government bureaucrats and politicians provided accounts of their involvement with the Westray mine and its aftermath. Typically, Crown ministers and their officials and senior politicians deflected blame and responsibility onto subordinates and miners, or claimed outright ignorance of the causes and consequences of the explosion. But Curragh Resources executives and mine managers did not testify, even though their refusals to do so were challenged by inquiry lawyers and bereaved family members, who sought to subpoena them as witnesses from outside the province of Nova Scotia (Richard 1997). The two Curragh Resources officials who did testify offered contradictory and provocative accounts of their roles and responsibilities, and denied any wrongdoing in either the circumstances leading up to the explosion or in their official reactions after the disaster. Clifford Frame, the CEO of Curragh Resources, belittled the inquiry, calling it a "railroad job and a farce" (*Chronicle Herald*, April 18, 1996: A1). He insists to this day that the explosion was a "simple accident." Former Premier Donald Cameron also claims that "Westray's truth" had nothing to do with him or his government's actions. He openly condemned the miners as the agents of their own deaths!

> The families... will never find any peace if they don't get to the truth, and that's why I am so upset that people wouldn't own up to what they were doing. And instead of briefly speaking about it and shoving it under the table. The bottom line is that the mine blew up on that morning because of what was going on in there at that time. That's the bottom line (Province of Nova Scotia, 1997, vol. 67, 14440)

The lack of cooperation and the evasive and forgetful testimony of corporate and state officials contrasted sharply with the clear and consistent accounts provided by mining experts, bereaved family members and miners. The former were critical of Curragh Resources' methods of operation and argued that the explosion was both predictable and preventable. The latter reported that they tried to convince the company to implement a plan to neutralize coal dust and to improve ventilation and roof conditions at the mine site. Some went directly to mining and health and safety officials, asking them to enforce compliance with the regulations, or to shut the mine down until it was safe (Comish 1993; Dodd 1999; Jobb 1999; Richard 1997). These officials, the inquiry was told, either ignored their complaints or stated that they lacked the power and authority to act on them. Family members of the dead miners, for their part, often left the hearings in anger, tears and disbelief. By July 22, 1996, the last day of hearings, the inquiry had heard testimony from seventy-one witnesses over seventy-seven days of meetings and produced 16,816 pages of official transcript.

By autumn of 1997, corporate executives and mine managers had still to account to the public for their actions and policies; they have steadfastly refused to do so to this day. After nearly eighteen months of judicial appeals and deliberations, Justice Richard abandoned the legal struggle to make Curragh Resources' executives and managers testify. He decided that there was enough evidence from other sources to draw conclusions about the failure of Curragh Resources officials to operate a safe mine, and he released his long-awaited report in December of 1997. Justice Richard was direct in his evaluation: "The Westray story," he wrote, "was a complex mosaic of actions, omissions, mistakes, incompetence, apathy, cynicism, stupidity, and neglect" (Richard 1997: 111). The politicians who negotiated the financing of the mine went "beyond the call of duty" to bring it into operation. Mine managers and executives encouraged a corporate mindset that placed production and profits ahead of health and safety. A culture of intimidation and recklessness, he opined, prevailed at the mine site, where occupational health and safety violations were normalized and even encouraged. The natural resources and labour departments failed to enforce proper oversight and allowed Curragh Resources to operate an unsafe mine. The formula for disaster, he argued, was abundantly clear: "management failed, the inspectorate failed, and the mine blew up" (Richard 1997: 12).

The final report contained seventy-four recommendations: it called for an overhaul of underground mining and health and safety regulations; changes to the regulatory regimes and their enforcement practices; guidelines for the conduct of elected politicians; and changes to the criminal law to make corporate officials more responsible and accountable for workplace violence. While Justice Richard hoped that his report afforded closure for the bereaved family members by absolving their loved ones of blame and dispelling the myth of accident, it did not lead to criminal convictions or civil actions against those identified as responsible for homicide in the workplace. As Justice Richard (1997: VIII) put it: "anyone who expects that this *Report* will single out one or two persons and assess total blame for the tragedy will be... disappointed." Indeed despite expenditures of $1.5 million for the RCMP investigation, $3 million for the criminal prosecution and $4.8 million for the public inquiry, no one has ever been convicted of a breach of occupational health and safety legislation or mining law, nor has anyone ever been convicted of a crime in the aftermath of the Westray disaster!

## The Bereaved and the Legacy of Westray

There is a chilling complacency behind the state's failure to address the harm, trauma and homicide of Westray. And there is a deep resentment in the voices of the bereaved for the failure of the authorities to return the bodies of their loved ones for proper burials; for their failure to provide a comprehensive statement of accountability for the explosion, including responsibility for individual wrongdoing in a criminal context; for ignoring the victims' experiences by failing to offer appropriate public recognition and apology; for not implementing an agenda of preventative reform; and for denying civil claims that would have eased the many torments of injustice over the past decade (Dodd 1999; Davis 2003). The brother of a dead miner put it forcefully:

> Those bastards did this and they are walking away from this.... You cannot touch Frame.... He's the ultimate. That's where the blame lies... and yet we cannot even get at the goddamn managers that were there. So I'm trying to see where this friggin' justice system fits in. It doesn't fit nowhere. Unless you happen to be a nobody, then they'll nail your ass right to the wall. It's odd. I just can't let it go that these people were able to kill twenty-six people and just walk away. (Cited in Dodd 1999: 238–39)

The latter decision, which was announced in August 2002, effectively meant that the government of Nova Scotia could not be held responsible under civil law for negligence in licensing and funding a dangerous mining enterprise, even though the public inquiry had indicated their culpability. The Supreme Court of Canada stayed the civil compensation suit against the Government of Nova Scotia on the grounds that the provincial government, which helped fund the Westray mine, was actually the miners' employer and had already compensated the Westray families under the *Workers' Compensation Act* (Province of Nova Scotia 1995).

Although some family members have moved on and have been able to create a positive legacy of Westray, many continue to experience traumatic losses: of identity, of trust in government, of family relations and of lives once lived. Two-thirds of fifty-two family members stated that they felt anger, frustration and bitterness over Westray, most of it directed against mine managers, politicians and regulators. Almost half of them recently said that the intensity of their feelings was "just as strong" now as in 1992 (Davis 2003: 6). For many, Westray is inexplicable — deaths without reason or meaning! For others, Westray is about "fate" or "murder for profit." But almost four out of five family members interviewed felt that corporate capital and the local state have learned little from the explosion. As Davis (2003: 9) observes:

> For some people, Westray is over... others though, cannot give up the fight. There are some among the families who need desperately to see justice prevail, to gain back the trust they had in mankind, or to know that there will never again be another Westray.

After ten and a half years of legal maneuvering, corporate denial and government deceit, those most closely affected by the disaster were effectively revictimized: lax regulatory responses and police practices, flawed technocratic criminal justice procedures, official bureaucratic secrets, miniscule workers' compensation awards and the failure to discipline those responsible have been so serious that they have transformed a physical disaster into a legal disaster, thereby undermining justice. A family member summed up her feelings as follows:

> I guess I never thought that anything like this could ever happen. I never thought that we could be made a mockery in public, and I never thought anybody could kill somebody and get away with it, so publicly. (Cited in Davis 2003: 6)

Another bereaved family member put it plainly:

> We were always taught if you keep your nose clean, keep your mouth shut, don't offend anybody, don't break the law, you'd be looked after. That's not true. Not only did we not break the law, not only were we church goers, not only were we good citizens, but we didn't do anything, and still there was no help and they did a hell of a lot to hinder us rather than help. (Cited in Davis 2003: 6)

Much of the sociology of law starts from the premise that law is invented and that it produces and transmits knowledge as truth. To some extent this is right, but a more complete analysis is that in the selection, construction and narrative formation of legal truth, the legal system circulates knowledge as truth through appealing to established conventions, norms and ideologies. In the Westray case, legal "truth" was constructed as a reflection of what Becker (1967) calls "a hierarchy of credibility." The mechanisms, instruments, techniques and procedures used to produce their version of the truth lay barely concealed beneath the surface of Westray's "official discourses and memories" and the state's legal maneuverings, diversions and refusals. They informed the ways in which the explosion was conceptualized and written about by the press and how "views from above" and "views from below" were registered, circulated, acknowledged and memorialized.

So how did the press respond to the Westray explosion? Can we uncover who framed the truth, why, with what consequences and with what relation to power? What is the best way to code the data produced by the press about Westray and its aftermath and study their news-truth? How can we measure the silences in these discursive transactions?

# 4. Studying the Press and Westray

## Introduction

The press were on the scene almost immediately after the explosion. Within hours, local and international journalists arrived at the tiny community of Plymouth, Nova Scotia, like a plague of high tech locusts, weighed down with portable computers, cellular telephones, cameras, microphones and truckloads of electronic gadgetry. As Jobb (1994: 52) recounts:

> The Westray explosion was the lead item on radio newscasts across the country. CBC Newsworld and local television stations were installing satellite dishes... so they could go live with updates... reporters for newspapers with Sunday editions were already typing stories into portable computers... CNN in Atlanta was beaming the story to the world.

The media reflected the volatility and chaos that characterized the explosion and its socio-legal aftermath. The demands imposed on them were well in excess of typical emergencies or daily tragedies. Existing routines, day-to-day policies and procedures, and accepted professional practices and protocols were disrupted. The psychological and social needs of the bereaved, of rescuers and of bystanders were subordinated to the priorities of investigative agencies, including the press. The entire community was invaded. At its peak, about two hundred journalists were reporting to national and international audiences (McCormick 1995: 212). Reporters parked on people's lawns, and doorsteps, commandeered local telephone lines and hounded the families of the missing and presumed dead. The relentless search for emotional detail, so common in media coverage of tragedies, resulted not only in bad feelings but in errors, some of which aroused shock and caused hurt. Bodies were misidentified. One mother received condolence calls all day when it was erroneously reported that her son's body had been one of the first eleven miners brought to the surface. Homes were entered without consent. Private conversations were recorded as public matters. Family names and local sites were misreported (McMullan 2001; Richards 1999).

> The CBC finally discovered the name of one of the men trapped below. They knew he was from Antigonish.... They called every person in the phone book with the surname who lived in Antigonish.... One of the people called was so angry he drove to

the community centre where the media was stationed.... He stormed over to the CBC contingent and said that if anyone called his family again, he would be back with a gun. (Cited in Richards 1999: 157)

Pack journalism and a tendency to report the event in terms of sheer sensationalism predominated in the immediate aftermath of the explosion. As one television reporter observed, journalists were fixated on feelings and were not looking for information.

The coverage centred around the press conference-driven thing. You know, the draegerman have moved four feet. We have established a fresh air base. We have discovered eleven bodies. And then there was a mad scramble to find the relatives of the eleven bodies. How do you feel about this? (Cited in Richards 1999: 155)

Not surprisingly, reporters were cursed by angry relatives of the dead and warned to "get out of town" by dismayed community leaders (McCormick 1995). Others were pelted with rocks by angry family members when they tried to enter the fire hall. As one reporter put it, they did not want you there [at funerals] and hated your guts" (cited in Richards 1999: 155). But were there different phases in the reporting of Westray? Did relations between the media, the company and the bereaved families change over time? How are we to understand the continuous registration and recording of "truth" surrounding the Westray disaster from 1992–2002?

## Genealogy and the Use of Content Analysis

Before analyzing the coverage of Westray it is important to discuss several methodological matters. I adopt a genealogical approach to the study of news telling because it accounts for the "constitution of knowledges, discourses, domains of objects, etc." (Foucault 1980a: 117) and identifies "local discursivities," where dispersion, disparity, difference and division construct the identity of truth. Genealogy considers the claims of "local, discontinuous, disqualified, illegitimate knowledges" against the claims of a "unitary body of theory" that filters hierarchies and orders them in "the name of some true knowledge" (Foucault 1980b: 83). Descent and emergence are two analytical tools that allow for the specificity of events to be recovered and for alternate accounts to be registered. Together they show how representations come together to form "fields of possible enunciations," "groups of concepts" and "ways of speaking" that are invested in systems of prohibition and valorization (Foucault 1988a: 193).

Descent identifies the dispersion associated with events rather than their unity. It rejects a linear, evolutionary framework of explanation in favour of a methodology that identifies deviations, false calculations and disparities, and one that questions presumed continuities (Foucault 1977: 146–47). Emergence emphasizes events as the "hazardous play of dominations," in a series of dynamic struggles that are marked by change and permanence. Emergence encourages the study of power and the institutionalization of rules, knowledge and truth, as well as the corollary processes of resistance and succession where those who are capable of seizing rules and meaning redirect them against those who imposed them in the first place (Foucault 1977: 151).

Genealogy focuses on the singularity of events in order to recover the heterogeneity of connections, strategies and forces that precipitate them and allow them to become self-evident. This process of decomposition and recomposition situates social issues in a "complex field of relations": the "elements" that brings news into existence, the "relations" that enable its survival and transformation and the "domains of reference" that the news inscribes externally, thereby making it intelligible for others (Foucault 1991c: 76–78). The key issue is how do people "govern themselves and others by the production of truth." How do they establish "domains in which the practice of true and false can be made at once ordered and pertinent" (Foucault 1991c: 79).

A genealogical approach to "news-truth" then introduces discontinuity into the taken-for-granted domains of press reporting and their readerly audience, focusing instead on news coverage as the effect of relations of power; it affirms Nietzsche's observation that the "value of truth" about the representation of events is a "perspective seeing," "a perspective knowing," formed by the "will to power" and the "will to knowledge." Genealogical analysis insists on an "ideal of truthfulness" that will not forget or falsify problems, processes and consequences. The values of truthfulness include the need to find out the truth, to hold on to it and to tell it to others and to oneself. As Williams (2002: 15) remarks, the pursuit of truth does not mean that we "believe any and every truth. It does mean that we want... to correct error, to avoid deceiving ourselves, to get beyond comfortable falsehood." Genealogy has a radical purpose: to discover how truth has been made tolerable without abandoning the idea of truth and truthfulness. To that end, this study of the press and Westray aims to deconstruct the production of truth and the exercise of power. It aims to be quite simply true, and the story as a whole aims to be truthful.

In order to analyze the news production of truth I adopt content analysis as a primary investigative tool for studying discourse. It may be defined as a "method of studying and analyzing communications in a systematic, objective, and quantitative manner for the purpose of measuring certain message variables" such as narrative themes, stories and the like (Dominick 1978: 106–107). It is particularly well suited to exploring the "classic questions of communications research: who says what, to whom, why, how and with what effect" (Maxfield and Babbie 2001: 329).

Content analysis is a relatively unobtrusive way of analyzing social relations through texts which, when combined with qualitative techniques, allows for patterns of meaning, tonality, continuity and discontinuity to be explored (Coffey and Atkinson 1996: 62; Manning and Cullum-Swan 1994: 464; Neuman 2003: 313; Riffe and Freitag 1997). Thus I utilize "two ways of seeing" in this study: on the one hand, I am systematic. I count images, types of news sources, narrative themes — the literal texts or apparent truths of news discourse. On the other hand, I emphasize the context of the production of texts and their signifying capacity for registering and reregistering latent messages in press reporting (Banks 2001; Jones 1996; Sturken and Cartwright 2001).

While quantitative and qualitative approaches are sometimes thought of as mutually exclusive, I view them as complementary and additive. Certain "textual terms" or "bundles of phrases" may portray a narrative that is clear and obvious to the reader, which, when retold over time, crystallizes into a powerful singular representation of an event. At the same time, this denotive configuration of storytelling may conceal discursive connotations by "writing them out," or marginalizing them in news narratives. For example, headlines may not accurately situate text-images and reflect the story content. Discursive images of causality or accountability for an event may or may not be shown. Subtexts may reinforce or subvert texts within stories (Gamson et al. 1992: 381). An examination of connotation reminds us that discourses are positioned within an ensemble of specific institutional practices that promote, prohibit and deny. Thus the configuration of context that constructs signs and signifies additional meanings must be added to the quantitative study of media messages. As van Dijk (1993: 254) puts it, the exercise of power is often cognitive; ·discourse analysis shows how "managing the minds of others is essentially a function of text and talk."

The presentation of news to readers invites the latter to survey images, captions and stories in an exercise where plot structure is integrated and repeated. Because this study is at "the representational level," it cannot evaluate the readers' reception of the news or the effects of content on the audience. Nevertheless, the categories I selected for quantification presuppose that media texts produce "preferred readings" that work towards the reader, promoting certain responses over others, in effect demarcating the life world of their audience (Eco 1979; Gitlin 1980). As Reiner (2002: 378) rightly observes, the strength of content analysis "lies in the precision of the statistical manipulation of data, but the categories used necessarily presuppose some theory of meaning, usually about likely consequences." Senders and receivers of news not only share assumptions and values; more importantly, they are each equipped with a consciousness constituted within dominant cultural understandings of reality. Readerly news texts can be contradictory, but the different realities of, for example, the mass murderer or the corporate killer are typically consti-tuted from a relatively stable field of possible readings. Astute audiences of mass mediated news can often "fill in" and "retell" the story, for example, of another schoolyard shooting or stalking crime. In this sense, one realm of media discourse is uncontested. Narratives appear and are appropriated as transparent descriptions of reality, not as interpretations. Editors, reporters and public opinion writers conflate sources with sincer-ity; they matter-of-factly state the one as the other. Thus in the reporting of the Gulf War, democracy and capitalism are narrated as synonymous, and the United States is represented as a nurturing nation spreading democracy to the Middle East! (Gamson et al. 1992: 382).

Media discourse, however, also involves "contested meanings," where news constructions intended for readers are ambiguous or resistant to hegemonic tales. Contested and uncontested domains can blur and re-form. For example, Gamson and Modigliani's (1989) study of nuclear disasters, shows how news narratives can shift from uncritical readings of nuclear power as representing technological superiority over nature to subversive readings that question the truths preferred by powerful corpo-rate and political actors. Senders and receivers of news may operate within a moving field of consensus and negotiation. While there are powerful constraints on narrativity in the news, success in manufacturing and manipulating preferred meanings does not always ensure dominance in the meanings constructed by readers. As Gamson et al. (1992: 383) con-clude, "challengers [environmental and anti-nuclear groups] were helped by the media," and "media norms and practices worked to some extent against" corporate and state narratives of nuclear necessity and mastery. Sending and reading media texts and images is an interactive process in which context, prior experience and social knowledge can lead to diverse codings and decodings of the news.

Contrary to some practitioners of content analysis, I do not claim that my analysis reveals an "objective structure" of meaning. Rather, I assume that there is a dialectic between text and reader: thus my results should be interpreted provisionally, as one truthful reading. As Counihan (1975: 36) observes, "a theory of content as discourses and texts is a partial but necessary precondition for an analysis of how dominant political and aesthetic ideologies are at work within the texts, dictating their silences as well as their statements." Media discourses are highly situated, often pseudo-descriptive accounts, that sustain everyday life by concealing the "social organization of their production and plausibility" and by produc-ing a "taken-for-granted reality" that effaces an examination of underly-ing assumptions. They reproduce ironic and paradoxical narratives (Ewick and Silbey 1995: 214). For these reasons I include excerpts from relevant discourses to provide reliability and to support my interpretations (Banks 2001; Jones 1996; Sturken and Cartwright 2001).

I followed four general guidelines in constructing discourse categories. I emphasized the independence of content categories in assigning values, and I was exhaustive in including as many sources and discourses as possible. Coded items were placed in only one category and for the most part, were treated as mutually exclusive; I adhered to a single classification schema so that different levels of analysis of categories were not combined. In addition to decoding news texts, I placed them in a critical interpretive framework. My aim was to explore the varieties of discourses and discursive regimes surrounding the reporting of Westray and to ask how far the conventions, presuppositions and regularities of news writing affected the ways in which the conduct of corporations, governments, the judiciary, the miners and their families were constituted, interpreted and registered as truth. So I studied news discourse as both an object of inquiry — the production of truth and social exchange through storytelling and inquiry — and as the production of scholarly narrativity; in the latter I offer an alternative story not readily present in journalists' accounts of Westray and after (Ewick and Silbey 1995: 202–204).

## News Sources and Sampling Strategies

The news sources that informed my analysis were drawn from newspaper reports published in the *Chronicle Herald* from February 9, 1992 to August 9, 2002. I defined my sample time period to include stories written three months before, and three months after, the ten-year anniversary of the explosion. This enabled me to observe patterns in the content, tone and form of news reporting over a decade and to analyze how the press "framed" events such as: (a) the immediate crisis aftermath of the explosion; (b) the regulatory investigative process under the *Occupational, Health and Safety Act* (Province of Nova Scotia 1996) and the *Coal Mines Regulation Act* (Province of Nova Scotia 1989); (c) the criminal investigation and the criminal justice process; (d) the provincial public inquiry and the public responses to it; and (e) the civil compensatory proceedings initiated by the Westray families against the government of Nova Scotia.

Some researchers in the field of media and corporate crime have used multiple newspapers and compared and contrasted regional and national coverage (Goff 2001; Lynch et al. 1989; Swigert and Farrell 1980; Molotch and Lester 1978). This has certainly produced interesting findings and enhanced validity and reliability of data (Cavender and Mulcahy 1998; Wright et al. 1995; Burns and Orrick 2002). Indeed, the inclusion of television sources has revealed fresh content and different discursive significations. Certainly an exhaustive sample of everything the national and provincial press presented on the Westray disaster might uncover new findings and alternative discursive connotations. But I want to emphasize that I familiarized myself with the press coverage from other local sources as well as with the coverage of another major Canadian national newspaper, the *Globe and Mail*, before I decided to analyze the total press coverage available from the *Chronicle Herald*. I am confident that my analysis identifies the key narratives that make up a complex set of discourses of media reporting about Westray.

The *Chronicle Herald* was especially important because it provided a longitudinal view of the local social climate and an enduring description of a society's response to a disaster. The newspaper afforded permanence and visibility to accounts that otherwise would have been transitory and opaque: it included public data, identification of community leaders and citizens and invaluable "features" (stories, letters, opinions, photographs, cartoons, announcements, etc.) which constituted and reconstituted sociocultural commonly held values and those which differed from the norm, about the explosion and its aftermath. The *Chronicle Herald* structured, in thought, memory and word, notions of self, social interaction and place, as well as the community's sense of expected conduct. It allowed me to understand how and why power/knowledge relations between reporters and news sources were structured into "truth regimes," and how and why these regimes were transformed as the community came to terms with the disaster.

I also selected the *Chronicle Herald* because it was (and still is) the predominant news organization in Nova Scotia. It has a readership of 325,000 — one-third of the provincial population — and it covers the entire province from Yarmouth in the south to Cape Breton in the north. It is the most widely read and circulated newspaper in Nova Scotia; it has not missed a publication day since 1875. The *Chronicle Herald* also has a history of covering local disasters: the Foord mine explosion in 1880; the sinking of the Titanic in 1912; the Halifax explosion in 1917; the Allan mine explosion in 1918; the Albion Macgregor mine explosion in 1952; and the Springhill mine disaster in 1957. It was especially useful as a source for studying Westray because (1) their journalists reported "on the spot" and did not rely on wire services to gather most of their information; (2) their journalists tracked the Westray explosion throughout the ten-year period and compiled an extensive archive of news reports, editorials, opinions, interview texts and public commentary; and (3) when compared to other regional or national newspapers, their reporters had an intimate knowledge of regional mining communities and local political and economic contexts.

The *Chronicle Herald* news reports were also easily accessible. For the years 1992–1998, they were available on CD-ROM at the university library. For the period from August 20, 1999, to August 9, 2002, they were obtained from the Virtual News Library, a web-based database that replaced previous compact discs. Both databases, however, did not contain news reports from January 1, 1999, to August 19, 1999, so these were obtained directly from the newspaper's corporate archive.

My goal was to obtain all news reports on the Westray explosion. I sampled broadly using "Westray" as my search term. I saved 2600 news items to disk, examined a high-reporting year and a low-reporting year, and developed a strategy for excluding certain news items based on relevance and length (Goff 2001; Chermak 1995; Wright et al. 1995; Ericson et al. 1989, 1991; Burns and Orrick 2002). Story relevance was determined by examining whether each story focused on the issues and events surrounding Westray. For example, some narratives pointed out parallels between the events and issues surrounding Westray and other corporate projects; other items made comparisons between Westray and other industrial disasters; and still other stories drew associations between political figures and state officials who were connected with Westray, although they did not focus their coverage on the Westray events proper. Since there was little text to code or analyze, these types of stories were omitted from the sample. On the other hand, the news reports were included in the sample when the connections, comparisons or associations between Westray and other topics, events and actors were extensive and continuous. In the cases where relevancy was difficult to decide, three researchers (including the author) formed a committee and made the final decisions.

Story length was determined by the column inches of each news report. Following Chermak (1995), Ericson et al. (1991) and Wright et al. (1995), I excluded news reports and capsules that were less than three column-inches because they did not contain enough information to analyze. Letters to the editor, however, were treated differently in the exclusion process. Letters-to-the-editor pages often included entries from several different citizens, but typically each entry was less than three-column inches and would have been excluded if I applied the "less than three column-inches" rule. Since I wanted the sample to reflect public opinion, I used the following rules. The first entry in the cluster that was more than three column-inches in length was included and all remaining entries were excluded. If none met the criteria of relevance and length, then the entire cluster was omitted.

Cartoons raised commentary about Westray. But they could not be analyzed as extensively as other news items. They tended to present singular images of Westray with clear and direct messages, but little text. They were coded by theme only. In the end, I excluded 698 news items, and retained a total working sample of 1,972 news reports, editorials, letters to the editor and cartoons. I divided the sample into three discernible time intervals: (1) February 9, 1992, to December 31, 1994; (2) January 1, 1995, to December 31, 1997; (3) January 1, 1998, to August 9, 2002. The first interval was selected because it was a time of intense public interest in Westray and because it was relatively free of the official probes into the explosion. The second interval was chosen because it included extensive coverage of the legal imbroglio surrounding Westray: the regulatory investigation, the criminal justice prosecution, the debate over the constitutionality of the public inquiry and the activities of the public inquiry. The third interval was adopted because it involved official and public responses to Justice Richard's report, coverage of the civil court proceedings initiated by the Westray families against Curragh Resources and the provincial government and reports about the ten-year anniversary of the Westray explosion, as well as the Supreme Court's long-awaited appeal decision on civil compensation for the bereaved families. These time intervals enabled me to calibrate the evolution of the news and then compare and contrast the quantity and quality of the coverage (Burns and Orrick 2002; Wright et al. 1995; Lofquist 1997).

## Coding the Data

I coded the content and source categories of each news report in the sample. I developed categories that measured the following general themes and questions:

- power/knowledge and newsworthiness: What issues and events and accounts surrounding Westray were considered to be credible and newsworthy?
- regimes of truth: Did power/knowledge relations structure the news as a discourse and create "statements of truth" about causes of the explosion and attributions of blame and responsibility?
- discourse and morality: Did news producers frame a moral vocabulary about the explosion? Did they discuss the harms and losses caused by the explosion?
- discourse, justice and denial: Did news providers construct images of social justice, criminal justice and reparation? What narratives were constructed about the official investigations into Westray and its aftermath? Were voices ignored, silenced or disqualified in the years of news reporting?
- the press, hegemony and corporate crime reporting: Did the news media examine the political economic context leading up to the explosion? Did the press simply follow their sources, or were they critical investigators of the event and its aftermath? Did reporters construct a law-and-order narrative about Westray? Was the news registered according to dominant hegemonic understandings of corporate capital and state power?

I then constructed a codebook listing the content categories, subcategories and definitions. The subcategories of each content category were numbered consecutively. In all there were seventy-eight content categories. For the content categories comprising the "vocabulary of corporate crime" (see the next section), the subcategory "no mention" was coded as "10" in order to measure the absence of coverage of each of the key indicators. Each news report was numbered consecutively and coded on a separate sheet. The sample (n = 1,972) was coded by two research assistants who worked together to ensure intercoder reliability by continually cross-checking each other's coding. In the few cases where there were conflicting interpretations, I made the final coding decision in consultation with the researchers.

Coding involved a constant process of reflexivity and revision. There were three types of codebook revisions. First, I revised content subcategories when they did not accurately reflect the content of the news sample. In most cases, the codebook was revised by adding subcategories so that they were mutually exclusive and exhaustive. For example, the content category "public inquiry" traced the inquiry through all of its stages of development from pre-public inquiry deliberations through public inquiry investigations, hearings, decisions, findings and recommendations, to inquiry follow-ups. However, I soon discovered that those categories overlooked the upsurge in news reporting in 1995–1996 that centred on the constitutional rulings surrounding the co-existence of the criminal trial and the public inquiry, so I revised this content category by adding "constitutional issues and rulings" as a subcategory.

Second, from time to time I revised subcategories so that they reflected the tone and language of news reports more precisely. For example, the category "morality" was divided into five subcategories: (1) accident; (2) immorality, but not criminality; (3) individual criminality; (4) systemic criminality; and (5) none mentioned. Systemic criminality, I discovered, was rarely discussed, but systemic immorality was framed in terms of government and corporate negligence or incompetence. These issues, moreover, were seen as by-products of capitalist social relations and bureaucratic social structures. These systems of power and authority were sometimes seen as immoral, but were seldom presented as criminogenic. Therefore, subcategory (4), systemic criminality, was redefined to include judgments of systemic immorality as evinced in the texts.

Finally, some new source content categories were added to the preliminary list. I soon discovered that journalists, in writing about Westray, used a variety of sources, even though some were used more often and considered more authoritative. In order to register and analyze the entire range of news sources, it was necessary to continually update the codebook, and in order to code the entire range of organizational positions held by news sources, it was necessary to reconfigure the source subcategories. This constant process of revision allowed me to capture the scope and character of what Becker (1967) calls "hierarchies of credibility," as they applied to the news production process proper.

## Content Categories and News Narratives

Some of my content categories were developed specifically for this research; others were borrowed from previous studies on the news media and corporate crime (Cavender and Mulcahy 1998; Goff 2001; Lofquist 1997; Swigert and Farrell 1980; Wright, Cullen and Blankenship 1995). The newsworthiness of Westray and the credibility attributed to different news sources were measured by three indices. First, the type of news coverage measured the length of each news report in order to gauge the scope of coverage. Subcategories included primary stories, which measured 5 or more inches of text in length; secondary stories, which measured between 2.5 and 4.9 inches of text in length; and tertiary stories, which measured between 1.6 and 2.4 inches of text in length (Lofquist 1997; Chermak 1995). Second, the placement of news reports was measured by examining where news reports were situated in the newspaper. Events that were featured on the front pages of newspapers were often the most important and newsworthy (Ericson et al. 1991; Chermak 1995). Subcategories included front page news; section A news, editorials, other sectional front page news (i.e., B1, C1, D1), and other inside page news (i.e., B2, C3, D4). Finally, the type of news story was measured by examining the newspaper's system of news identification. Subcategories included ordinary news reports, feature stories, editorials, commentaries/opinions, entertainment stories, cartoons and other news stories. Together, then, these variables were used to measure the newsworthiness of Westray as an event and to track the dynamics of news reporting over time.

In order to study the degree to which news reports focused on the key issues and events I developed the following threefold measure. Was the focus: (a) primary and direct, with the Westray case in the foreground; (b) secondary, with the Westray case in the background and indirectly discussed in relation to other narratives about the explosion, legal action, miners and their families, etc.; or (c) tertiary, with the Westray case merely mentioned as an instance of a larger narrative about politics, law, regional economies or other mining disasters.

I also constructed three content categories to track the regulatory, criminal justice, and public inquiry probes over time, and measure the volume and intensity of news coverage about each investigation. The regulatory investigation was tracked as follows: (a) investigation stories that reported on the detection of violations under the *Occupational Health and Safety Act* (Province of Nova Scotia 1996), and the *Coal Mine Regulation Act* (Province of Nova Scotia 1995); (b) charge stories that reported on the fifty-two allegations brought against Curragh Resources and its officials; (c) outcome stories that reported on the actions taken as a result of (a) and (b); and (d) follow-up stories that revisited the regulatory investigation process and reflected upon the actions taken and not taken.

The criminal justice investigation was tracked according to the following: (a) investigation stories, which reported on the collection of evidence and the construction of a criminal case against Curragh Resources and its officials; (b) arrest stories, which reported on the apprehension of Curragh officials for criminal negligence causing death and manslaughter; (c) charge stories, which documented the charges against Curragh Resources and its officials; (d) pretrial stories, which examined the legal deliberations concerning evidence, witnesses, strategies and procedural rules; (e) plea stories, which reported the pleas entered by Curragh Resources and its officials; (f) trial stories, which tracked the testimony, movements and decisions of the trial; (g) appeal stories, which reported on all matters of appeal throughout the court process and afterwards; and (h) follow-up stories, which reviewed and reflected on the criminal justice process and its aftermath.

The public inquiry was tracked according to the following: (a) constitutional stories that addressed the constitutionality of the public inquiry going forward at the same time as the criminal trial; (b) pre-public inquiry deliberation stories that discussed the scope of the inquiry, the nature of evidence, documents and types and numbers of witnesses present at the inquiry; (c) hearing stories that reported on witness testimony and evidence; (d) procedural ruling stories that reported on Justice Richard's decisions regarding admissibility of evidence, witness standing, and location of hearing sites; (e) result stories that reported the principle findings of cause, blame, harm and responsibility for the explosion; (f) recommendation stories that documented the proposed policy and legal reforms flowing from the work of the public inquiry; and (g) follow-up stories that reviewed and commented on all aspects of the public inquiry and its aftermath.

I included twelve source categories in order to gain insight into whose accounts about Westray were most represented in the news. These include: (1) corporate sources — executive officers, managers, other Westray "officials," and other unknown Westray sources; (2) regulatory sources — members of the Department of Labour and the Department of Environment; (3) police sources — chiefs and superintendents, sergeants and constables, special investigators, spokespersons and unknown police sources; (4) legal sources — judges, crown prosecutors, defence lawyers, union lawyers, Westray Families Group lawyers, government lawyers, civil lawyers and other legal sources ; (5) expert sources — government-paid consultants, privately paid consultants, independent consultants and unknown expert sources; (6) citizen sources — miners, victims' spouses, victims' relatives, community members, draegermen, Westray Families Group and protest groups; (7) political sources — the prime minister, the Premier, members of cabinet, members of the political parties in power and in the opposition, local mayors and other political party affiliates; (8) government sources — administrators, ministers (other than the labour minister), boards and agency officials and unknown government officials; (9) labour sources — members of labour federations, the United Steel-workers of America Union, unknown union officials and other labour sources; (10) private sources — mine analysts, mine competitors, outside media sources and other private sources; (11) other sources — medical, religious and academic; and (12) other unknown sources — often represented by the ambiguous phrase, "sources say."

Each news report was also coded according to its discursive content. These narratives were derived in part from the secondary literature on Westray (McMullan 2001; McMullan and Hinze 1999; Goff 2001; Richards 1999; McCormick 1995) and in part from my pretest of random reporting years. Seven news discourses were identified:

1. the discourse of natural tragedy, where the Westray explosion was constructed as a "natural accident" framed by a vocabulary of loss, grief, bravery and sacrifice said to be typical of miners and their communities coping with unexpected disaster;
2. the moral outrage and reform discourse, where Westray and its aftermath were constituted as a morality drama involving denunciation and pleas for social reformation;
3. the law and order discourse, where Westray and the social responses to it were demarcated as violations of law, with precise offender/victim relationships and various justice outcomes;
4. the political and regulatory failure discourse, where the explosion was narrated as an event framed by negligent state officials and incompetent safety inspectors;
5. the discourse of legal tragedy, which represented the Westray explosion and its aftermath as primarily a juridical phenomenon emphasizing procedural rules, courtroom conflicts and judicial appeals and decisions;
6. the political economy discourse, which highlighted the public and state economic context surrounding the Westray explosion and its aftermath, and related how it precipitated the explosion and the responses to it; and finally
7. "other" indexed news reports that were not represented by any of the above themes. Each content and source category was then examined on a time interval basis that allowed for the study of trends, frame developments, discursive transformations and narrative absences.

Finally, the extent to which journalists developed a "vocabulary of corporate crime," by which I mean news narratives that delineated cause, attributed blame and responsibility, demarcated harm and used a crime language to frame Westray and its resolution was measured by the following indices (Wright, Cullen and Blankenship 1995; Lofquist 1997; Cavender and Mulcahy 1998; Goff 2001; Burns and Orrick 2003; Swigert and Farrell 1980). First, what causes did journalists attribute to the explosion? Was the explosion a result of (a) worker negligence; (b) a natural disaster; (c) corporate criminal conduct; (d) systemic failures; or (e) specific individuals behaving irresponsibly. Second, how did journalists characterize the harm caused by the explosion? Was harm considered as (a) direct — focused on the miners killed in the explosion; (b) indirect — focused on the grief and loss experienced by family and friends of the deceased miners; or (c) community-based — focused on the impact of the explosion on the regional economy and community relations? Third, how did journalists write about intent as it related to criminal culpability? Was intent (a) overt — as when corporate officials, regulatory personnel and local politicians ignored the safety complaints of miners, experts, and industry; or (b) indirect — as in instances where mine officials failed to monitor and maintain a safe worksite or properly train miners for work underground? Fourth, how did journalists constitute blame and responsibility for the explosion? In their news narratives were the responsible parties registered as (a) mine managers; (b) regulatory personnel; (c) politicians and/or corporate executives; (d) miners; or (e) a combination of the above? Fifth, how did journalists frame discussions of story resolution in their news narratives? Did they register justice in their news representations as (a) criminal resolution; (b) civil compensation; (c) regulatory reform; (d) public exposé and apology; or (e) legal and political reform? Finally, how did the press frame morality in the news coverage? Was Westray viewed as (a) an accident beyond human control and morally neutral; (b) an act of omission or commission by individuals who were immoral, but not criminal; (c) a crime caused by criminals; or (d) an act that was the structured outcome of a political-economic system that was organizationally criminogenic?

So how did the local press register and re-register Westray's truth? What were their procedures for elucidating relevance and believability? To what degree was the media a "site of struggle" over contested claims about the causes, conditions and consequences of Westray?

# 5. The Press and the Production of Westray's Truth

## The Social Form of News Representation

What form did the news coverage of Westray take? From 1992 to 2002, the press produced mostly primary type stories (72 percent), followed by secondary (19 percent) and tertiary (9 percent) forms of coverage. The number of primary stories remained consistent over time: 68 percent in interval one, 79 percent in interval two and 66 percent in the last interval.[1] Fully three-quarters of the coverage focused directly on the issues and events central to the Westray explosion and its aftermath; while 15 percent emphasized secondary issues and events, and 10 percent had a tertiary focus. Consistent with the type of news coverage, the number of stories with a primary focus in the coverage was highest in the second interval (83 percent); intermediate in the first interval (73 percent); and lowest in the third interval (67 percent). News narratives indexing a secondary focus in the coverage were consistent for the first two intervals at 13 percent, and then they increased in the third interval to 23 percent of all news. News coverage of an indirect tertiary focus was also highest during the first interval (14 percent), surpassing coverage with a secondary focus, but then it declined dramatically to 4 percent in the years 1995–1997, and returned to only 10 percent of the coverage in the third interval.

Almost half of the news produced about Westray was recorded in the years between 1992 and 1994. As McCormick (195: 210–11) notes, at the time when the "Westray disaster" became the "Westray case," the coverage dropped considerably, from an average of about twenty-five articles a day to about two a day. Yet Westray still evoked continuous interest, even after initial saturation coverage. Indeed 54 percent of all the news reports were located in Section A of the newspaper, and an additional 22 percent were front-page stories.

While the volume of news diminished over time from 939 news reports in interval one to 362 items in interval three, the percentage of news stories placed in section A of the newspaper increased: 49 percent in the first interval; 54 percent in the second interval, and 70 percent in the third interval. About one-quarter of all stories were front-page news from 1992 to 1997, but the percentage declined substantially to about 10 percent from 1998 to 2002. Seven in ten news stories were ordinary reports, followed by court reports (11 percent), editorials (9 percent), feature stories (3 percent), cartoons (3 percent), other (2 percent) and entertainment (1 percent) (Table 1).

TABLE 1 — Type of News Stories, 1992–2002

|  | N | % |
|---|---|---|
| Ordinary News Reports | 1337 | 67.8 |
| Editorials/Commentaries/Opinions | 173 | 8.8 |
| Letters to Editor | 101 | 5.1 |
| Feature Stories | 50 | 2.5 |
| Entertainment | 17 | 0.9 |
| Cartoons | 49 | 2.5 |
| Other | 30 | 1.5 |
| Court Reports | 215 | 10.9 |

N = 1972

Ordinary news reports remained fairly consistent in the coverage, except during the second interval, when they dropped from 75 percent to 54 percent of all types of news stories. Relatedly, the number of court stories increased from 6 percent in the first interval to 22 percent in the second interval. Editorials and letters to the editor accounted for only 14 percent of the news coverage; this remained consistent over the years, except for a slight increase to 18 percent in the third interval (Table 2).

TABLE 2 — Type of News Stories by Time Interval

|  | 1st | 2nd | 3rd |
|---|---|---|---|
| Ordinary News Reports | 699 | 364 | 274 |
|  | (74.5%) | (54.2%) | (75.5%) |
| Editorials/Commentaries/Opinions | 86 | 45 | 42 |
|  | (9.2%) | 6.7%) | (11.6%) |
| Letters to Editor | 38 | 40 | 23 |
|  | (4.0%) | (6.0%) | (6.4%) |
| Feature Stories | 18 | 30 | 2 |
|  | (1.9%) | (4.5%) | (0.6%) |
| Entertainment | 7 | 6 | 4 |
|  | (0.7%) | (0.9%) | (1.1%) |
| Cartoons | 18 | 29 | 2 |
|  | (1.9%) | (4.3%) | (0.6%) |
| Other | 19 | 9 | 2 |
|  | (2.0%) | (1.3%) | (0.6%) |
| Court Reports | 54 | 148 | 13 |
|  | (5.8%) | (22.1%) | (3.6%) |
|  | N = 939 | N = 671 | N = 362 |

Westray news was primarily constructed by journalists. Reporters accounted for 84 percent of the news in interval one, 87 percent in interval two; and 88 percent in interval three. Editors produced 4 percent of the news in the first interval, 6 percent in the second interval and 7 percent in the third interval. News wire services accounted for 8 percent of the news production in the first interval, 3 percent in the second interval and 2 percent in the third interval. Opinion stories, editorials and commentaries accounted for 9 percent, 7 percent and 12 percent of all Westray news written over the three intervals respectively; columnists and editorial writers were even less frequent news producers. Cartoonists were alternative producers of news who provided satirical images rarely expressed in other news texts. But they never accounted for more than 4 percent of the news produced in any interval (Table 3).

---

TABLE 3 — Type of News Story Producers by Time Interval

---

|  | 1st | 2nd | 3rd |
|---|---|---|---|
| Reporters | 726 | 538 | 294 |
|  | (83.8%) | (86.9%) | (88.3%) |
| Editors | 38 | 34 | 24 |
|  | (4.4%) | (5.5%) | (7.2%) |
| Newswire | 69 | 20 | 5 |
|  | (8.0%) | (3.2%) | (1.5%) |
| Columnists/Editorial Writers | 15 | 3 | 8 |
|  | (1.7%) | (0.5%) | (2.4%) |
| Cartoonists | 18 | 24 | 2 |
|  | (2.1%) | (3.9%) | (0.6%) |
|  | N = 866 | N = 619 | N = 333 |

---

The focus, story placement and type of story indicate an important development brought about by the public inquiry. As the inquiry unfolded, newsworthiness increased, as evinced by the rise in the production of primary focus stories between the first and second intervals (73 percent to 83 percent), even though the total volume of news reporting declined from 921 to 642 stories. The proportion of section A stories also increased in the second interval, while the proportion of front-page stories remained consistent at about 24 percent. During the third interval, however, primary focus coverage declined (83 percent to 67 percent), as did front page coverage (24 percent to 11 percent). However, secondary- and tertiary-focused coverage increased (13 percent to 23 percent and 4 percent to 10 percent respectively), as did section A coverage (54 percent to 70 percent). So the end of the public inquiry in late 1997 seems to have precipitated a quantitative downturn in the newsworthiness of Westray and, as we shall see, a re-registration of the news that was qualitatively different.

## Discursive Denotations and Connotations

How was Westray discursively constituted? What were the dominant narratives and truth statements about Westray? How did they signify the explosion and its aftermath? Legal narratives were predominant, accounting for 31 percent of the coverage. Reporters commonly covered the regulatory process, the criminal justice proceedings and obstacles, and the constitutional debates over the criminal trial and the public inquiry, as well as the conflicts between the company and the legal system. The following excerpts demonstrate the technical and formal tone typical of legal news writing.

> The owners of the Westray coal mine will be in court today in a bid to keep about 120 documents out of the hands of investigators probing last May's fatal explosion. Westray coal and its parent company Curragh Incorporated of Toronto, contend the documents are privileged correspondence between the firms and their lawyers and must remain confidential. (*Chronicle Herald*, October 15, 1992, A4)

> At least three officials of the Department of Labour will be questioned about missing Westray documents at a special session this month.... Sources connected with the Westray inquiry say the witness list includes.... The department's lawyer, Marian Tyson, and Stewart Sampson, an occupational hygienist who was responsible for collecting documents for the inquiry, will also testify. The inquiry ordered all Westray documents to be turned over three years ago. But some of Mr. White's notebooks, which outlined his activities before the explosion, only surfaced two months ago. (*Chronicle Herald*, July 1, 1995, A2).

These narratives were often formulaic, and coded in play-by-play, "he said/she said" statements that narrated the courtroom dramas of the day and mirrored the legal logics of accusation and defence. The polemical style worked to suppress the violent effects of the explosion, to exceptionalize its meaning, to reframe human suffering as legal tragedy and to distance the corporation from the consequences of the event.

> the Supreme Court of Canada ruled Thursday that public hearings, stalled by a Nova Scotia Appeal Court ruling in the fall of 1992, can go ahead despite the fact a criminal trial is under way. The inquiry will also be able to order testimony from former Westray managers Gerald Phillips and Roger Parry, who are being tried in Pictou on charges of manslaughter and criminal negligence causing death. "Holding the public hearings prior to, or concurrently with, the

criminal trials would not violate the fair trial rights of the two accused managers," the court said.... In some circumstances, proceeding with the public inquiry may so jeopardize the criminal trial of a witness called at the inquiry that it may be stayed or result in important evidence being held to be inadmissible at the criminal trial, the court said... [Justice Minister Bill Gillis] wants to be sure that allowing the inquiry to proceed will not cause a mistrial. (*Chronicle Herald*, May 5, 1995, A1)

The next most common discourse used to denote Westray as news was that of natural disaster (17 percent). The general impression conveyed by this discourse was that the harm, violence, death and suffering were the result of capricious causes. A certain "mystique" about coal mining was advanced. Coal was "in the blood" and dying hard underground was a brave but necessary choice that miners knowingly made and that their families accepted. But, in contrast to previous research that reported this discourse as hegemonic (McMullan and Hinze 1999; McCormick 1995; McMullan 2001; Goff 2001, Richards 1999), it was of secondary significance overall when considering the ten-and-a-half-year reporting period (Table 4).

TABLE 4 — Type of News Discourse, 1992–2002

|  | N | % |
|---|---|---|
| Natural Disaster | 341 | 17.4 |
| Moral Outrage and Social Reform | 121 | 6.1 |
| Law and Order | 190 | 9.7 |
| Political and Regulatory Failure | 259 | 13.1 |
| Legal Tragedy | 617 | 31.3 |
| Political Economy | 264 | 13.4 |
| Other | 178 | 9.0 |

N = 1972

The following are exemplars of this discursive framing of Westray.

Stan MacPherson, 71, of Goshen, Guysbourgh County, described the grief of relatives when they heard the grim news. Mr. MacPherson... said the scene was one of "sadness"... Grief counselors and clergy met with family and friends of the trapped miners to prepare them for a possible tragedy.... Reverend Angus J. MacLeod... said the relatives had been supporting each other. The time together should help relatives with the tragedy, he said. "They've gotten tremendous strength from one another," he said. They're learning to accept whatever comes. (*Chronicle Herald*, May 11, 1992, A1)

Even as friends and mourners paid their last respects at the graveside to seven of eleven men killed in last weekend's Westray mine explosion, there was more tragic news... rescuers... discovered the bodies of three more miners... Pictou County's mining communities have borne their burden day after day with dignity, fortitude and grace [they] showed us what it is to hope, to have faith. (*Chronicle Herald*, May 14, 1992, C1)

The Westray bump is a terrible reminder of the enormous sacrifice made by generation after generation of brave men to mine Nova Scotia's deep coal seams.... This is an awful legacy. But it is also an awesome testament to the courage of those who go down to the deeps... advanced technology... hasn't changed the equation. It is still brave men toiling in the face of unseen danger in the dark. The risks are still there; the men still go knowingly to meet them. (*Chronicle Herald*, May 11, 1992, C1)

Methane... has always posed a lethal threat to coal miners working in underground tunnels. The gas is being blamed for the explosion which rocked the Westray mine Saturday morning and claimed the lives of at least 11 miners. Dr. Arthur MacNeil says methane and carbon monoxide, both gases monitored at Westray, can cause death through inhalation. The time it takes to kill a victim depends on the gas volumes present in the air inhaled. (*Chronicle Herald*, May 11, 1992, A1)

Political economy narratives followed at 13 percent of the coverage. They narrated Westray as a disaster in the making conditioned by economic forces and the will to power. In this reporting, a different drama was being circulated. Metaphorically speaking what was being actualized through language was a recognition of political opportunism, economic brokering and failed governance.

A downcast Premier... went on national television to promise a full inquiry into the disaster that killed 26 miners.... Nothing it appeared, could stand between Westray and Pictou County coal. Rival mine promoters were sent packing, repeated warnings of unsafe conditions in the mine were dismissed as political opportunism, fears of lost mining jobs in Cape Breton were ignored, and federal bureaucrats who felt Ottawa was offering too much financial backing were attacked in the press. Westray was a creature of politics. In the mid 1980s the government of Cameron's predecessor, John Buchanan, was looking for a firm to develop a mine... the timing was perfect, Cameron — whose riding borders the Westray site — and two other Tories in the Pictou area were re-elected helping the Buchanan government cling to a four seat majority.... Westray remained the government's favourite son after Cameron reached the Premier's office in early 1991. (*Chronicle Herald*, May 23, 1992: C1)

The... miner who admitted covering up safety violations before an inspector arrived said he feared for his job in a region where unemployment is chronic and options are limited.... Merrick has spoken of the "unraveling fabric" of safety in the Westray mine, how job fears, intimidation, production and mounting roof problems all conspired to detract from the miners' greatest threats — gas and coal dust.... Witnesses have all danced around it, but no one has yet made a link between inspector MacLean's apparent unwillingness to act and the provincial government then headed by Phillips' friend and local Tory hero, Donald Cameron. It was Cameron... who helped secure $100 million in government financing and loan guarantees for a project which at least one company had already deemed a sure money-loser... area politicians pursued the Westray project as a saviour for the hard-pressed region and possibly for their own political fortunes. (*Chronicle Herald*, March 30, 1996, B2).

Federal bureaucrats opposed the [Westray] project and a deal was only reached after lengthy negotiations.... Mr. Merrick said the evidence has shown that politics played a role in Westray. "Political interference can be in a variety of forms" he said. "It can be a direct phone call or it can be a way of doing things that changes a result. I think the evidence has pretty clearly indicated that there obviously were political influences of that more general kind." (*Chronicle Herald*, June 14, 1996, A1)

Overall, however, news narratives were not usually critical of corporate acts of commission or omission. Instead, metaphors conveyed to their readers a sense of congruence with corporate experience. They valorized the business world inclusively and not as a normatively ascribed "other." Nevertheless a consistent percentage of news characterized the explosion in a discourse of political and regulatory failure that emphasized some state negligence and official incompetence (13 percent).

The provincial NDP caucus heard a three-and-a-half hour "nightmare" account of working conditions at the Westray mine from about 50 miners.... "It really was a nightmare account of the absence of health and safety provisions, procedures and protection that is intended under our health and safety legislation," NDP leader Alexa McDonough told reporters after the meeting. (*Chronicle Herald*, May 23, 1992: A2)

Mr. Cheverie… said he was a little anxious about approaching Mr. MacLean [inspector], since he was in a position of authority. But Mr. Cheverie… was worried about roof conditions and lack of stone-dusting, which reduces the explosiveness of coal dust. "I asked him point blank if he had the power to shut the mine down if they weren't doing things properly," he said. And he told me no. He told me I had the right to refuse work if I felt it was unsafe… but he led me to believe that he would be no help to me. "Here I thought I would find an ally in safety and really, it was presented to me that I didn't have anyone to turn to." Under the province's Occupational Health and Safety Act, a Labour Department inspector can shut down a workplace until safety hazards are corrected. (*Chronicle Herald*, January 19, 1996, A1)

Cameron told the inquiry he had no knowledge of safety problems at Westray, and no inkling the province's mine engineers and mine inspectors were not doing their jobs…. But there would have been no mine in the first place without massive government backing, and that's a subject Cameron knows well. As Buchanan and MacKay were happy to point out to the inquiry, he was the driving force behind those deals. Ottawa, after tremendous lobbying from the Nova Scotia government, guaranteed an $85 million bank borrowing and committed millions more to subsidize the loan's interest rate. Cameron's industry department provided a $12 million loan. The provincially owned electrical utility agreed to buy 700,000 tones a year of Westray coal to burn at its Trenton power plant…. Cameron apparently did not foresee himself being on the hot-seat four years ago, when he gave Justice Richard a wide mandate to determine what caused the explosion…. Tough questions were only beginning to be asked about working conditions at Westray and the Cameron government's role in promoting and inspecting the mine. (*Chronicle Herald*, May 31, 1996, C1).

Yet the press was much less likely to portray Westray in a language of moral approbation: only 6 percent of the coverage signified strong condemnation for the loss of life and for the aftermath of legal failure; one in ten news narratives cast Westray in a law-and-order discourse signifying criminal culpability.

Some interesting patterns, however, emerge when we examine news production in more detail by time periods and include a qualitative analysis of connations. News reports that mapped the political economic context accounted for 25 percent of the coverage during the first interval. If we add narratives that registered connections between the explosion and political and regulatory matters, then 38 percent of the sample in interval one recorded Westray in a language of political suspicion and critical reservation. Legal narratives were also fairly high as a percentage of all stories in the first interval (21 percent); news that emphasized the capricious, tragic and human interest dimensions of the natural disaster amounted to about the same proportion of the coverage in the same time interval (21 percent) (Table 5).

TABLE 5 — Type of News Discourses by Time Interval

|  | 1st | 2nd | 3rd |
| --- | --- | --- | --- |
| Natural Disaster | 205 | 59 | 79 |
|  | (21.8%) | (8.7%) | (21.8%) |
| Moral Outrage and Social Reform | 39 | 29 | 53 |
|  | (4.1%) | (4.3%) | (14.6%) |
| Law and Order | 48 | 118 | 24 |
|  | (5.1%) | (17.6%) | (6.6%) |
| Political and Regulatory Failure | 129 | 83 | 47 |
|  | (13.7%) | (12.4%) | (13%) |
| Legal Tragedy | 193 | 304 | 120 |
|  | (20.7%) | (45.4%) | (33.2%) |
| Political Economy | 231 | 16 | 17 |
|  | (24.6%) | (2.4%) | (4.7%) |
| Other | 94 | 62 | 22 |
|  | (10.0%) | (9.2%) | (6.1%) |
|  | N = 939 | N = 671 | N = 362 |

On the surface, in the early coverage, there was discursive plurality — a complex overlapping of different truth regimes, from natural disaster to legal tragedy and structured violence. But on closer reading, what followed from much of this coverage was not so much an actual reporting on governance and safety as it was the mobilization of safety issues to construct a different type of discourse — one where the voices of the workers were overshadowed by the voices of politicians and experts, and where inanimate chemical and geological forces, rather than organizational decisions, were blamed for the explosion. Hints of corporate wrongdoing and regulatory impropriety were crowded out by discursive narratives that emphasized the anonymity and unpredictability of the explosion, and that coded and recoded the emotional overtones of the disaster: resetting the explosion, applauding the rescue efforts, exploring the structure of family feelings and drawing out expressions of community pain and suffering.

The media stayed with the emotional and tragic because they were easy to stage and manage, and because this type of story line fit well with the organizational practices of news workers. These stories were simple to process: they could be moved quickly into news copy. Standard leads about family suffering, accidents and mining communities, for example, were easily obtained, composed and followed up over time, making it seem as if reporters were systematic and objective (Chibnall 1977; Fishman 1980; Rock 1973; Sumner 1990; Walters et al. 1989). The preferred news response to misfortune and victimization was what Knight (1980: 179) calls a "disavowal of knowledge of human causes." Yet something else was also at play at the edges of the news-making process — the signalization of the Westray explosion as a "possible crime" against employees, the effect of which was working to reconfigure popular beliefs and locate potential threats and dangers inside the boardrooms of business and the corridors of the state. In short, news reporting attributed a "high signal value" to the explosion, establishing it as a focal point of tragic concern as well as political anxiety.

This overall pattern changed during the second interval. Reporting of political and regulatory negligence, and of political economy explanations, dropped dramatically to 15 percent of the coverage. Legal narratives, however, more than doubled to 45 percent, and that reporting encoded an emerging law-and-order discourse that accounted for about 18 percent of all news produced between 1995 and 1997. While the press characterized Westray as representing a potential violation of criminal and regulatory law, they simultaneously formatted the structural context of the explosion to the margins of the coverage:

> "Complaining about safety didn't do much good at Westray," Wayne Cheverie, an underground industrial mechanic told the inquiry into the May 1992 disaster that killed 26 men. He and other employees knew that complaining about safety could "bring undue hardship on yourself," and that those who did were often reprimanded or intimidated. Mr. Cheverie testified that parts of the Plymouth, Pictou County, mine were so deep in explosive coal dust that miners were told not to drive equipment through for fear of getting stuck.... Nova Scotia mining regulations require operators to keep coal dust neutralized with limestone powder. But Mr. Cheverie... said he'd only seen it done once.... "Gerald Phillips and Roger Parry ran the mine with an iron hand," he said.... He said any decisions on production or maintenance were made by them and they would at times override other supervisors, "using their same style of intimidation." (*Chronicle Herald*, January 18, 1996, A1)

The law and order narrative signified wayward, "respectable" individuals, but it conveyed the message that systemic problems were rather minor in precipitating the explosion. The cause of the disaster and the "cover-up" afterwards was about "bad people" functioning poorly in an otherwise "good system" of resource extraction and production. In focusing on specific actors and legal charges that alleged that they did not take steps to prevent an explosion, the corporation was not discursively framed as an economic enterprise with business goals, standard operating procedures, systems of authority and ideologies. Instead micro-level pathology or immorality type explanations worked to convert structured organizational dynamics and memories into atomized actors and actions without collective directions, plans or responsibilities (Barlow et al. 1995: Welch et al. 1998). The corporation as a social entity was framed in the discursive background, while middle-level managers and inspectors were celebrated in the coverage. What followed from this rather restrictive news reporting lens was a remarkably banal and benign signification of corporate culpability that inhibited critical reflections on the motives of the powerful and encouraged an "audience effect" to see Westray as an exercise in legal gymnastics governed by procedural signs, symbols and words (Walters et al. 1989).

> Curragh Incorporated has replaced Westray general manager, Gerald Phillips, who was mine manager for Westray coal when the May 9th explosion occurred.... Mr. Phillips is one of four Westray officials charged with infractions of provincial occupational health and safety laws following the disaster. He left his post as mine manager following the explosion. (*Chronicle Herald*, December 26, 1992, A6)

> Prosecutors and the RCMP were mum Wednesday on the fate of their bid to view documents seized last month... on October 12th, the rcmp seized a lawyer's notes of an interview conducted with Roger Perry, one of two former Westray managers facing criminal charges in the May 1992, explosion deaths of 26 coal miners. The notes were placed in a sealed envelope pending a court hearing to determine whether solicitor-client privilege protected them from disclosure. (*Chronicle Herald*, November 10, 1994, A3)

> At least three officials of the Department of Labour will be questioned about missing documents at a special session this month.... The inquiry ordered all Westray documents to be turned over three years ago. But some of Mr. White's note books, which outlined his activities before the explosion, only surfaced two months ago. (*Chronicle Herald*, July 1, 1995, A2)

In the third time interval, the discourses of legal tragedy and law and order declined to 33 percent and 7 percent respectively. The natural disaster discourse, on the other hand, re-asserted itself up from 9 percent to 22 percent of the coverage; at the same time, the form and sentiments of the discourse remained similar. Stories were remembered painfully; the tragic was recaptured by displaying "selective sampling tactics" that memorialized the event as a natural catastrophe, reframing it by comparison to other mining explosions. The sentiment behind these narratives was certainly understandable; the public wanted to know how people were coping in the aftermath! But these depictions were often overwhelming: they were framed by a frequent association of limited signifiers that produced a singular symbolic representation of natural causation, shared grief and moral altruism without a human cause. Essentially, this discursive coverage projected the idea of a capricious world impinging on a stable societal order — one whose essential features, while expanded, remained relatively similar from year to year (Ricoeur 1980).

Narratives emphasizing political incompetence and negligence, on the other hand, increased only slightly from 12 percent to 13 percent of the news coverage. One in five news narratives questioned the role of the state and corporate capital in the explosion, but they did not highlight safety and regulatory failure in the coverage in any of the time intervals (3 percent, 6 percent, and 3 percent) and least of all in the later years, when there was strong evidence to encode it. But the press did start to register a measure of moral disapproval of Curragh Resources and especially of the government for their involvement in the explosion and afterwards; this increased from 4 percent of the coverage in interval two to 15 percent in interval three (see Table 5). Consider the following two news excerpts:

> The [miners] should not have to wait any longer for someone to actually be responsible. That somebody should be cabinet.... It has continued, shamefully to dodge the ultimate responsibility: paying a share of damages to the injured parties. (*Chronicle Herald*, January 1, 1998, D1)

> One would think both he [Clifford Frame] and Mr. Pelley would feel morally bound to help the inquiry under Justice Peter Richard to get to the bottom of this tragedy.... Instead their steadfast refusal to do the right thing resulted in a complex legal row.... This isn't too much to ask, of any decent human being. (*Chronicle Herald*, June 18, 1997, C1)

Juridical investigations into the Westray explosion received considerable news coverage as subsets of the total news making: the public inquiry generated 419 stories (47 percent); the criminal investigation evinced 340 stories (38 percent); and the regulatory investigation produced 137 stories (15 percent) for a total of 896 news reports (Table 6).

TABLE 6 — News Coverage by Type of Investigation

|  | N | % |
|---|---|---|
| Regulatory Investigation | 137 | 15.29 |
| Criminal Justice Investigation | 340 | 37.95 |
| Public Inquiry Investigation | 419 | 46.76 |

N = 896

News about the regulatory investigation was brief and limited when compared to criminal justice and public inquiry coverage. In the regulatory investigation, most news reporting centred on the investigation itself (35 percent), as well as the charges against Curragh Resources and its officials under the *Occupational Health and Safety Act* and the *Coal Mines Regulation Act* (64 percent). Strikingly, only 1 percent of the news coverage focused either on the outcome of the regulatory investigation or on the wisdom of aborting the regulatory charges in favour of criminal action (Table 7).

TABLE 7 — News Coverage by Stages of Regulatory Investigation

|  | N | % |
|---|---|---|
| Regulatory Investigation | 48 | 35.1 |
| Regulatory Charges | 88 | 64.2 |
| Outcome of Regulatory Action | 1 | .7 |

N = 137

Similarly, most narratives on the criminal justice process focused on the pre-criminal investigation (39 percent), the arraignments and hearings (11 percent), the charges of manslaughter and criminal negligence causing death (15 percent) and the trial (19 percent). Coverage then quickly declined as witnessed by the small percentage of appeal (14 percent) and follow-up stories (2 percent) (Table 8). In the public-inquiry investigation most news also centred on the preliminary deliberations (31 percent), the constitutional rulings (27 percent) and the hearings proper (28 percent) (Table 9). Only 5 percent of the news coverage encoded the findings, recommendations and decisions of the investigation; there were few follow-up stories or commentaries signified as news (Burns and Orrick 2002; Chermak 1994; Wright et al. 1995; Randall 1987, 1988).

TABLE 8 — News Coverage of Westray by Stages of Criminal Justice Investigation

|                                      | N   | %    |
|--------------------------------------|-----|------|
| Arrest                               | 2   | .6   |
| Charges                              | 51  | 15.0 |
| Pretrial/Arraignment/Hearing         | 37  | 10.9 |
| Plea                                 | 1   | .3   |
| Trial                                | 63  | 18.5 |
| Appeal                               | 47  | 13.8 |
| Follow-up Stories                    | 5   | 1.5  |
| Pre-Criminal Justice Investigation   | 134 | 39.4 |

N = 340

TABLE 9 — News Coverage by Stages of Public Inquiry Investigation

|                                 | N   | %    |
|---------------------------------|-----|------|
| Pre-public Inquiry Deliberations| 128 | 30.5 |
| Public Inquiry Investigation    | 39  | 9.3  |
| Hearings                        | 116 | 27.7 |
| Public Inquiry Decisions        | 2   | .5   |
| Findings                        | 7   | 1.7  |
| Recommendations                 | 8   | 1.9  |
| Follow-up Stories               | 5   | 1.2  |
| Constitutional Issues/Rulings   | 114 | 27.2 |

N = 419

## The Relative Absence of a Crime, Law and Order Discourse

Did journalists mobilize a discourse of corporate crime as defined in the previous chapter? For the most part they did not construct a discourse about the causes of the explosion. In the first time interval 70 percent of news narratives, followed by 72 percent in the second interval and 85 percent in the third interval, did not mention cause, even though more and more information concerning the origins of the explosion was uncovered in the courts and in the public inquiry. There was, however, a minority reporting that framed the explosion in a language of individual causation and moral anxiety. During the first time interval, 16 percent of news coverage identified individual wrongdoing as the cause of the explosion. This increased to 21 percent in the second interval and then fell to 7 percent in the years from 1998 to 2002. The following excerpts are illustrative of the "personality" approach to news representation.

Jack Noonan, the Labour Department's executive director of occupational health and safety, was let go... the Nova Scotia Federation of Labour said it had lost confidence in Mr. Noonan's ability to serve as the province's top safety official. Claude White, the former director of mine safety, testified last month he was unable to convince Mr. Noonan to commit more money to monitoring Westray... the department had referred Mr. Noonan to the Nova Scotia Commission on Drug Dependency. He was undergoing treatment when the explosion occurred. Inquiry lawyer John Merrick has referred to Mr. Noonan's problem only as a "disability." Union official Robert Wells has been more blunt, telling the inquiry Mr. Noonan had a "drinking problem on the job." One of Mr. White's memos to Mr. Noonan, outlining the need for engineering assistance to monitor Westray, came back with sarcastic comments scrawled in the margins. "It's his style to be abrasive," noted Mr. White. (*Chronicle Herald*, June 10, 1996, A5)

Mr. McLean... told the inquiry no miners came to him with complaints about working conditions. That flew in the face of the sworn testimony of Mr. Comish and other miners.... When confronted with their evidence, Mr. McLean either denied making the statements or couldn't recall the discussions. (*Chronicle Herald*, May 16, 1996, A5)

The testimony of John Smith... has been filled with rambling, convoluted answers, frequently punctuated by short bursts of laughter and lengthy anecdotes but often little substance.... Inquiry Commissioner Justice Richard also seemed incited by Smith's answers and asked him for a simple yes-or-no response.... Inquiry lawyer John Merrick suggested that the Labour Department might have been manipulated by Westray managers. Under questioning... Mr. Smith reluctantly agreed. (*Chronicle Herald*, May 19, 1996, A1)

Organizational causes, on the other hand, were seldom embedded in the news narratives: 6 percent, 4 percent and 8 percent in respective intervals. Workers were also rarely represented as causal agents and the natural-disaster vocabulary was mostly circulated in the first two years following the explosion, after which it declined as a cause of the explosion. Taken together, cause was marginal to the overall coverage which often featured disaster writing without an explanation (Table 10).

TABLE 10 — Attribution of Cause in News Coverage by Time Interval

|  | 1st | 2nd | 3rd |
|---|---|---|---|
| Worker Negligence | 1 | 9 | — |
|  | (0.1%) | (1.4%) |  |
| Natural Disaster | 64 | 6 | 4 |
|  | (6.7%) | (0.9%) | (1.1%) |
| Crime | 3 | 2 | — |
|  | (0.3%) | (0.3%) |  |
| Organizational Causes | 58 | 25 | 28 |
|  | (6.3%) | (3.9%) | (7.8%) |
| Individuals | 151 | 136 | 24 |
|  | (16.4%) | (21.2%) | (6.7%) |
| None Mentioned | 644 | 464 | 304 |
|  | (70.2%) | (72.3%) | (84.4%) |
|  | N = 921 | N = 642 | N = 360 |

The press did try to narrate the harm of the explosion and its aftermath. During the first and second time intervals, 18 percent and 27 percent of the news narratives constituted the *direct* harm of the explosion. Stories focused on death and emphasized the sacrifice and suffering that bereaved families endured with grace and dignity. News stories also documented the communal and residual harms of the explosion. Emotive narratives were deployed to set a somber mood and to draw the distant reader back to the event and on to the ceremonies of remembering.

> The black granite memorial with 26 beams of light commemorating the victims will replace a wooden cross erected in a field near the mine.... It is difficult for family members to cope with this tragedy.... If you've got somebody dead, you want to go and mourn with him.... "Where are you going to mourn?" Mr. MacKay said, "The bodies are still underground, you cannot get down to them." (*Chronicle Herald*, May 8, 1993: A4)

Year after year, the public was invited "to feel" the narrative of remembering and allow their perceptions of the tragedy to be constituted by it. As Kellner (1990) notes, news informs but it also permeates, organizes and defines interaction with the life-world of the reader, promoting in this case a preferred universe of shared dramatic meaning around redundant horror. Still the most striking finding was the degree to which harm was not signified at all. Indeed, this absence intensified with time, from 63 percent, to 68 percent, to 72 percent of the coverage not representing it at all (Table 11).

TABLE 11 — Attribution of Harm in News Coverage by Time Interval

|  | 1st | 2nd | 3rd |
| --- | --- | --- | --- |
| Direct | 168 | 172 | 43 |
|  | (18.2%) | (26.8%) | (11.9%) |
| Residual | 80 | 24 | 46 |
|  | (8.7%) | (3.7%) | (12.8%) |
| Community | 91 | 7 | 13 |
|  | (9.9%) | (1.1%) | (3.6%) |
| None Mentioned | 582 | 439 | 258 |
|  | (63.2%) | (68.4%) | (71.7%) |
|  | N = 921 | N = 642 | N = 360 |

When harm was discussed, it was usually framed in the vocabulary of sudden shocking death, and then later in a reflexive language of justice deferred or denied. Consider the news report in the immediate aftermath of the explosion compared to the one in the context of the public inquiry.

> Underground mining in Nova Scotia... has long been a story of great human courage pitted against great natural hazards. And too often it has also been a history of hope and fortitude and heartbreak in the face of unbearable tragedies. So it was again in Plymouth, Pictou County, this weekend, when a methane bump early Saturday buried 26 miners underground.... And the dimension of the tragedy, as of last evening, was truly heart-rending. The bodies of 11 miners were found by rescuers Sunday afternoon.... It's no exaggeration to say that all of Nova Scotia is now waiting and praying for the men still imprisoned underground. (*Chronicle Herald*, May 11, 1992, C1)

> Nova Scotia has failed, in ways big and small, to account for, or to hold anyone accountable for the horrible explosion.... The inquiry... was set back by court challenges, false starts, and a whole string of witnesses more interested in pointing fingers than in explaining their roles in the operation or regulation of the mine. Nor has the inquiry been successful in compelling Cliff Frame to testify.... The vague criminal charges first laid against mine managers Roger Parry and Gerald Phillips were thrown out of court by one judge. A second judge, presiding at a trial on redrafted charges, stayed the proceedings over the drearily familiar issue of Crown disclosure (or lack of it). Earlier this year, the Supreme Court of Canada ordered a new trial, which has yet to begin. Take a look at the big picture, then, and you begin to understand the frustration of the people who lost loved ones five years ago.... We

should pardon the families, then, for the ongoing skepticism with which they view the tragedy and its aftermath. (*Chronicle Herald*, May 8, 1997, C1)

Reporters wrote even less about intent. It was not mentioned in 87 percent of the news coverage in the first interval, 79 percent of the news coverage in the second interval, and 93 percent of the news coverage in the third interval. When it was narrated, intent was usually constructed as overt: 10 percent in interval one, 17 percent in interval two, and 7 percent in interval three. The following story raises the spectre of corporate negligence and intentional wrongdoing.

> The ventilation system was routinely tampered with, and the... sealed-off area was leaking gas.... you have the ingredients for a methane explosion.... Merrick, however, dismisses that theory as "simplistic," noting poor ventilation and high methane levels plagued the mine for months. It also ignores the fact bosses bullied miners who complained about working conditions or refused to do hazardous work. And it conveniently overlooks the role of coal dust, which most mining experts agree gave the Westray explosion its lethal, mine wrecking power. Nova Scotia law demands that coal dust be mixed with powdered limestone — called stone dust — to make it incombustible. But Westray miners say managers never established a stone dusting routine and allowed a thick layer of coal dust to build up underground. Lack of stone-dusting is the main allegation underlying the criminal charges against Phillips and former underground manager Roger Parry. (*Chronicle Herald*, June 1, 1996, C1)

In the following news report, wrongdoing is acknowledged, but the explosion is seen as an act of omission.

> Mine executive Collin Benner took his share of responsibility Tuesday for the Westray disaster and said others should too.... "My fault was that I assumed that was working." He says he was "somewhat seduced by technology" and assumed what was billed as state-of-the-art equipment at the mine was functioning properly.... Mr. Benner said the responsibility for mine safety lies with management at the site, supervisors and workers. Government regulators may not have had a direct responsibility but should have been "the watchdogs and guardians" over safety and welfare of workers.... [Benner] wonders whether he could have done "something more." (*Chronicle Herald*, July 10, 1996, A1)

But these discursive signifiers were relatively rare in the news representations. Indeed intent was still rather marginal in the coverage from 1995 to 1997; when the juridical investigations were front and centre, the press reported overt and indirect intent in only 21 percent of the news reports about Westray (Table 12).

TABLE 12 — Attribution of Intent in News Coverage by Time Interval

|  | 1st | 2nd | 3rd |
|---|---|---|---|
| Overt | 92 | 111 | 6 |
|  | (10.0%) | (17.3%) | (1.7%) |
| Indirect | 25 | 23 | 18 |
|  | (2.7%) | (3.6%) | (5.0%) |
| None Mentioned | 804 | 508 | 336 |
|  | (87.3%) | (79.1%) | (93.3%) |
|  | N = 921 | N = 642 | N = 360 |

Attributions of blame and responsibility were also occasional in the news writing. There was no discussion of these in 78 percent of the coverage in the first interval, 73 percent of the coverage in the second interval and 85 percent of the coverage in the third interval. When they were mentioned, the accounts were ambiguous as to who should be held accountable. In the first time period, the press attributed blame to Westray managers 9 percent of the time, to senior politicians and corporate executives 5 percent of the time and to a combination of sources (i.e., mine managers and politicians, but not corporate executives) 6 percent of the time. In the second time interval, attributions of blame and responsibility shifted from senior politicians and corporate executives to middle-level mine managers and regulatory officials, who together were identified in about 25 percent of the coverage. Interestingly a "blame the victim" narrative, which often typifies media accounts of corporate and state wrongdoing, was not seriously represented in the iconography of responsibility in the news coverage of Westray (2 percent). Even narratives that attributed blame and responsibility to "respectable personalities" were recast in the last four years of the coverage with over 85 percent of the news reports not presenting them or attributing organizationally based blame at all (Table 13).

Acknowledging story closure, where the press identifies social rules and reconfirms community norms in their plot lines, was also rather absent when compared to conventional crime reporting. Ninety-two percent, 77 percent and 65 percent of news narratives by period did not encode it at all. In the first interval, when the news coverage attributed resolutions, it usually favoured criminal outcomes. Forms of resolution were more prominently displayed in the news coverage in the second time

TABLE 13 — Attribution of Blame and Responsibility in News Coverage by Time Interval

|  | 1st | 2nd | 3rd |
|---|---|---|---|
| Company Management | 82 | 71 | 7 |
|  | (8.9%) | (11.1%) | (1.9%) |
| Government Regulatory Personnel | 19 | 31 | 3 |
|  | (2.1%) | (4.8%) | (0.8%) |
| Senior Politicians and/or Corporate Executives | 46 | 6 | 11 |
|  | (5.0%) | (0.9%) | (3.1%) |
| Miners | 1 | 9 | 11 |
|  | (0.1%) | (1.4%) | — |
| Multiple Attributions | 53 | 58 | 32 |
|  | (5.8%) | (9.0%) | (8.9%) |
| None Mentioned | 720 | 467 | 39t |
|  | (78.1%) | (72.8%) | (85.3%) |
|  | N = 921 | N = 642 | N = 360 |

period. There were increases in narratives expressing criminal resolution (from 4 percent to 7 percent), regulatory resolution (from 1 percent to 3 percent), and the use of the public inquiry to arrive at truth and justice (from 0 to 9 percent). The following are exemplars of the press's attributions of these forms of resolution:

> Methane caused the Pyro blast, which killed 10 men. The same potentially explosive gas... ignitcd in Pictou County's Westray mine... triggering a powerful coal-dust explosion that left 26 dead. The disasters occurred at collieries with a history of safety problems, and in jurisdictions where government inspectors were lax about enforcing the law, and forgiving when they detected violations. At Pyro and Westray alike, corners were cut in the push for coal production and profit. And criminal investigations were launched after both disasters. But that's where the similarity ends. Last week three former Pyro executives were jailed after pleading guilty to charges that included lying about safety conditions, failing to report high levels of methane and operating without an approved ventilation plan.... Meanwhile the troubled, drawn-out prosecution of Westray's top managers — Gerald Phillips and Roger Parry — remains tied up in the appeal courts. Westray's owner Curragh Resources is named in the charges but is now bankrupt.... Nova Scotia and Kentucky have different laws governing mine safety, and different agencies for investigating and prosecuting such offences. Despite those differences, the

convictions in the Pyro case stand in stark contrast to the Westray prosecution, where so far justice has proven elusive. (*Chronicle Herald*, June 22, 1996)

Imposing stiffer penalties, including jail terms, is one of the best ways to improve mine safety.... These penalties apply to individuals, not just companies. "All of a sudden, you get the attention of supervisors," he [Don Mitchell — mining consultant] said. "Word soon gets around that even company directors could be subject to a personal fine or time in jail. It's amazing what a good stick will do to get people to pay attention," he said. At the Westray mine... there were numerous safety violations. Fifty-two charges under the Occupational Health and Safety Act were laid in the fall of 1992, but were subsequently dropped the following spring.... But jail terms for safety violations are rare in Nova Scotia.... The province last month introduced a new health and safety act, expected to become law later this year. The legislation will increase maximum penalties to a $250,000 fine and two years in prison. (*Chronicle Herald*, January 12, 1996, A5)

The Westray report has given Genesta Halloran something she'd waited more than five years for. "It does definitely give you some type of closure.... It's almost like a peace of mind knowing we were right all along.... It was preventable.... Those men lost their lives senselessly. It didn't have to happen. That was the biggest thing I wanted him [Justice Richard] to come out and say." (*Chronicle Herald*, December 2, 1997, A1)

TABLE 14 — Attribution of Resolution in News Coverage by Time Interval

|  | 1st | 2nd | 3rd |
|---|---|---|---|
| Criminal Resolution | 36 | 46 | 2 |
|  | (3.9%) | (7.2%) | (0.6%) |
| Civil Resolution | 7 | 8 | 58 |
|  | (0.8%) | (1.2%) | (16.1%) |
| Regulatory Resolution | 9 | 20 | 3 |
|  | (1.0%) | (3.1%) | (0.8%) |
| Political and Legal Reforms | 19 | 17 | 63 |
|  | (2.1%) | (2.6%) | (17.5%) |
| Public Inquiry | — | 58 | — |
|  |  | (9.0%) |  |
| None Mentioned | 850 | 493 | 234 |
|  | (92.2%) | (76.9%) | (65.0%) |
|  | N = 921 | N = 642 | N = 360 |

Overall the press was rather reactive in writing closure into their narratives. They mobilized a minor vocabulary of crime only after official legal processes authorized this as a legitimate discourse. It was not until the third interval that reporters seriously signified political and legal reforms (from 3 percent to 18 percent), and civil liability (from 1 percent to 16 percent) as community resolutions to the Westray tragedy in their news narratives (Table 14). The following are exemplars of this news talk:

> His message [John Merrick — inquiry lawyer], over and over, has been what he and the judge see as the report's most crucial findings and recommendations. "We have got to sit down and rethink the whole approach of how we go at this as regulators. We can't have a hands-off approach," he says, referring to enforcing safety laws in workplaces in general, not just coal mines. "And you've got to have people qualified to do that, people skilled enough to do that, people who are prepared to rock the boat.... We don't rock the boat enough around here.... Change must start at the top — from the premier down... everyone in the chain of command has to be dedicated to excellence, and must demand nothing less from those below them." (*Chronicle Herald*, December 6, 1997, C1)

> "Every time someone wants to cut corners or bend the rules, we will remind them," he said. "There will never be another Westray, and this government will not allow it." (*Chronicle Herald*, December 2, 1997, A1)

> Downe sidestepped the issue of compensating them [Westray families] out of court.... The plain-as-your-nose answer is the government cannot, morally or legally, wriggle out of compensating the Westray victims' families... it [the government] will lose most if it chooses litigation. That way the price will not just be more money, but more shame, more bitterness, more distrust. (*Chronicle Herald*, December 20, 1997, B11)

Nor, it must be said, was the press generally inclined to write in the language of moral approbation. Indeed, stories not mentioning it increased from 73 percent to 86 percent in the news coverage. The press either linked morality to tragedy or framed moral judgements within a "personality paradigm." At the beginning they were inclined to represent individuals as immoral but not as criminals. This pattern, however, changed in the second interval: attributions of individual criminality jumped to 23 percent of the coverage and attributions of non-criminal immorality declined to less than 1 percent of the news reporting. Journalists certainly instituted a new iconography of images about corporate and state conduct.

> Frame, let's face it, launched a vile argument against testifying before the inquiry. His lawyers said compelling Cliff to appear would somehow infringe his liberty. Huh? This is a man who spent about $100 million of public money to open a mine that blew up, killing 26 men.... That could be described as an infringement of their liberty too. (*Chronicle Herald*, July 18, 1997, C1)

> The prospect of the courts never passing judgement on the guilt or innocence of Westray's bosses is what the Martins and other families fear most.... "I think justice probably means a lot of things to a lot of people, but to most, someone has to be held legally accountable.... Twenty-six people are dead... so why aren't people being held accountable?" (*Chronicle Herald*, May 3, 1997, A1)

But in interval three there was a dramatic reversal in the attribution of individual criminality (down to 1 percent) but a moderate increase in the attribution of systemic immorality and criminality (up from 3 percent to 10 percent) in the news coverage (Table 15).

TABLE 15 — Attribution of Morality in News Coverage by Period

|  | 1st | 2nd | 3rd |
|---|---|---|---|
| Accident | 75 | 5 | 1 |
|  | (8.1%) | (0.8%) | (0.3%) |
| Immorality, but not Criminality | 77 | 5 | 8 |
|  | (8.4%) | (0.8%) | (2.2%) |
| Individual Criminality | 61 | 145 | 5 |
|  | (6.6%) | (22.6%) | (1.4%) |
| Systemic Criminality | 36 | 19 | 35 |
|  | (3.9%) | (3.0%) | (9.7%) |
| None Mentioned | 672 | 468 | 311 |
|  | (73.0%) | (72.8%) | (86.4%) |
|  | N = 921 | N = 642 | N = 360 |

Some comments exemplify these findings:

> "I think it's a natural tendency in a bureaucracy as a large organization like this government.... to want to close ranks where there are fingers being pointed," says Halifax lawyer David Roberts.... "There have been times when you would have expected certain witnesses to accept responsibility for the failure of the system," he added in an interview. "It can't be denied that the system failed

here. And they wouldn't do it." That reluctance frustrated relatives of the explosion victims, who have been waiting for answers
for more than four years. (*Chronicle Herald*, June 29, 1996, B1)

He [Albert McLean] would have had to be a hero to merely do his
job. Like most of us, he wasn't. Nor did these departments end up
in such a bureaucratically depraved state because the individuals
in them weren't doing their jobs, as the report implies. The
nature of civil service depends on the political culture in which it
operates. Civil servants' motivation, their sense of public service,
depends largely on the clarity and purposefulness of their tasks.
Bureaucratic lassitude, on the other hand, is most often a reaction
to the politicization of their tasks — interference for partisan
purposes, promotions based on politics not merit, the rules being
bent for political reasons. There need be no direct order given
from the political level. With time and usage, the limits are
understood. (*Chronicle Herald*, December 12, 1997, C1)

Unlike news reporting of conventional crime, which dramatizes harm,
blame, cause, intent and moral resolution as a representational reality, the
press coverage of Westray did not lead to what Cavender and Mulcahy
(1998) call a "crime news frame" (see also Burns and Orrick 2002; Goff
2001; Lofquist 1997; Wright et al. 1995, for comparative case examples).
Instead their coverage sent the message that Westray was sensationally out
of the ordinary. While there were critical connotations conveyed, we shall
see that these terms carried implications of scandal, not serious legal
offence. Even then, about three-quarters of all news reports did not evince
moral condemnation of Westray or of the social reaction to it.

## News Sources, Claims Making and News Registration

Discursive developments were closely tied to the press's ability to maintain communicative relationships with news sources. As Van Dijk (1991:
124) notes, "the news media do not passively describe or record news
events in the world, but actively reconstruct them, mostly on the basis of
many types of source discourses." Overall, the news coverage was domi-
nated by legal, political and government sources. In the first interval,
political and government representatives were frequently reported in the
news (32 percent), followed by citizen (16 percent), legal (14 percent),
corporate (13 percent) and regulatory (9 percent) sources. By the second
interval, political, corporate and government officials were cited less often
and the press used more and more legal experts (39 percent) to make the
news. Political (18 percent) and government sources (15 percent), however, returned to representational prominence in the news in the third
time interval (Table 16).

TABLE 16 — Sources of the News by Time Interval

|  | 1st | 2nd | 3rd |
|---|---|---|---|
| Company | 155 | 60 | 11 |
|  | (10.6%) | (6.9%) | (2.1%) |
| Regulatory | 130 | 69 | 47 |
|  | (8.9%) | (8.0%) | (9.0%) |
| Police | 46 | 27 | 4 |
|  | (3.1%) | (3.1%) | (0.8 |
| Legal | 201 | 335 | 112 |
|  | (13.7%) | (38.7%) | (21.5%) |
| Expert | 52 | 57 | 15 |
|  | (3.6%) | (6.6%) | (2.9%) |
| Citizen | 230 | 119 | 67 |
|  | (15.7%) | (13.7%) | (12.8%) |
| Politician | 269 | 48 | 92 |
|  | (18.4%) | (5.5%) | (17.6%) |
| Government | 196 | 75 | 79 |
|  | (13.4%) | (8.7%) | (15.1%) |
| Labour | 87 | 20 | 43 |
|  | (6.0%) | (2.3%) | (8.2%) |
| Private Industry | 38 | 30 | 40 |
|  | (2.6%) | (3.5%) | (7.7%) |
| Other | 42 | 14 | 11 |
|  | (2.9%) | (1.6%) | (2.1%) |
| Unknown | 16 | 12 | 1 |
|  | (1.1%) | (1.4%) | (0.2%) |
|  | N = 1462 | N = 866 | N = 522 |

A more detailed examination of political and government sources reveals that cabinet sources declined over the decade from 30 percent in the first interval to 14 percent in the last interval. Opposition politicians, however, were regular and frequent claim makers: 49 percent in interval one, 44 percent in interval two, and 83 percent in interval three (Table 17). State ministers were also steadfast news makers while government administrators and appointed board and agency officials constituted either minor or dramatically declining news sources (21 percent, 1 percent and 1 percent). Unknown government sources (i.e., "a source close to the minister said," "an unnamed official in the Department of Justice announced") were consistently coded: they increased in the news-making process from 25 percent in interval one to 51 percent in interval three (Table 18).

TABLE 17 — Elected Political Sources and Positions by Time Interval

|  | 1st | 2nd | 3rd |
|---|---|---|---|
| Premier and Members of Cabinet | 80 | 19 | 13 |
|  | (29.7%) | (39.6%) | (14.2%) |
| Members of Party in Power | 11 | 7 | 2 |
|  | (4.1%) | (14.6%) | (2.2%) |
| Opposition MLAs | 131 | 21 | 76 |
|  | (48.7%) | (43.7%) | (82.5%) |
| Prime Minister | 6 | — | — |
|  | (2.2%) |  |  |
| Mayors | 33 | 1 | 1 |
|  | (12.3%) | (2.1%) | (1.1%) |
| Other | 8 | — | — |
|  | (3.0%) |  |  |
|  | N = 269 | N = 48 | N = 92 |

TABLE 18 — Government Sources and Position s by Time Interval

|  | 1st | 2nd | 3rd |
|---|---|---|---|
| Administrators | 9 | 10 | — |
|  | (4.6%) | (13.3%) | — |
| Government Ministers | 97 | 40 | 38 |
|  | (49.6%) | (53.4%) | (48.1%) |
| Government Board and Agency Officials | 41 | 1 | 1 |
|  | (20.8%) | (1.3%) | (1.3%) |
| Unknown Government Officials | 49 | 24 | 40 |
|  | (25.0%) | (32.0%) | (50.6%) |
|  | N = 196 | N = 75 | N = 79 |

TABLE 19 — Company Sources and Positions by Time Interval

|  | 1st | 2nd | 3rd |
|---|---|---|---|
| Executive Officers | 55 | 23 | 2 |
|  | (35.5%) | (38.4%) | (18.2%) |
| Management | 38 | 24 | 5 |
|  | (24.5%) | (39.9%) | (45.4%) |
| Westray Officials | 57 | 13 | 4 |
|  | (36.8%) | (21.7%) | (36.4%) |
| Unknown Company Source | 5 | — | — |
|  | (3.2%) |  |  |
| N = 155 | N = 60 | N = 11 |  |

While company sources had a minor representation in the news, corporate executives and officials were cited rather often in the early reporting period (36 percent and 37 percent respectively); both company sources and executives and officials used their authority to protect and manage corporate credibility with the press (Table 19).

Especially in intervals two and three, they, along with mine managers, steered the news in the direction of natural tragedy (Comish 1993; Richards 1999; McMullan and Hinze 1999; McMullan 2001).

> Outside the briefing room, a handful of relatives of the trapped men, wrapped in blankets to ward off the chilly night air, stood outside the adjacent Plymouth Fire Hall, where the family members await news from the mine.... There was no word on cause of death, pending autopsies.... Mr. Benner [Curragh Resources — president of operations] denied all charges that the mine was not a safe operation. These widespread accusations are "absolutely false," he said. "Some people are assuming that human error is the only possible cause of such a tragedy. There are miners in Pictou County who will tell you that is just not so. Mother nature cannot always be predicted or controlled." (*Chronicle Herald*, May 11, 1992, A1)

Regulatory agencies were also a consistent news sources in the news-making process. Government ministers responsible for these agencies (75 percent) displayed their authority to define and sustain a perception of competent health and occupational oversight. By the second interval their credibility with the media was waning. The labour minister, in particular, was targeted as a news notable under suspicion.

> Former provincial labour minister Leroy Legere can't recall if he questioned a department inspector about the follow-up on a critical order issued 10 days before the Westray explosion.... "I don't specifically remember asking him [Albert McLean — inspector], 'Why didn't you follow up?'" said Mr. Legere.... Mr. Legere said he wished his memory was better about some of the events surrounding Westray. "I have to admit there are many things in that period of time that are just not there. There were a lot of things that went on. There was a lot of information that came. Some of it has stayed fairly vividly, some of it has not." Among the information forgotten or never received was a September 1992 memo from Claude White, then director of mine safety, to Mr. Legere. The memo is a request for an investigation into the competency of mine managers... and supervisors.... The memo alleges the six men "are unfit to discharge their duties by reason of incompe-

tence, misconduct or gross negligence." (*Chronicle Herald*, June 13, 1996, A3)

When the minister resigned, there followed a decline in the use of regulatory sources in the news-making process until interval three.

During the years from 1995 to 1997 press coverage shifted to mine managers and mine inspectors as news sources (52 percent). Both in terms of spoken about or spoken to, they framed communication with the press from a distance and denied claims that could be coded within a law-and-order news narrative. By interval three, managers and inspectors too had diminished as sources in the news-making process, from 35 percent to 28 percent, and 17 percent to 0 percent respectively. A new labour minister however was a major news maker (51 percent), and his branch of government, along with the Department of Natural Resources, was depicted by the press in increasingly critical terms (Table 20).

TABLE 20 — Regulatory Sources and Positions by Time Interval

|  | 1st | 2nd | 3rd |
|---|---|---|---|
| Ministers | 98 | 24 | 24 |
|  | (75.3%) | (34.8%) | (51.0%) |
| Management | 6 | 24 | 13 |
|  | (4.7%) | (34.8%) | (27.7%) |
| Mine Inspectors | — | 12 | — |
|  |  | (17.4%) |  |
| Labour and Environment Dept. Officials | 26 | 9 | 10 |
|  | (20.0%) | (13.0%) | (21.3%) |
|  | N = 13 | N = 69 | N = 47 |

Some examples of this process are the following:

> The government should hire more inspectors and improve training to ensure the safety of Nova Scotia's workplaces, according to an assessment carried out in response to the Westray inquiry.... Justice Richard's report found Labour inspectors were "derelict" in their duty to enforce mining regulations and ensure Westray operated safely.... The report raises concerns about inadequacies in inspection and enforcement.... The department's resident expert, Claude White, was fired in December after he was severely criticized in the Westray report. A Department of Natural Resources official has since been seconded to Labour. (*Chronicle Herald*, April 17, 1998, B7)

> The government must move quickly to strip the Natural Resources Department of all responsibility for mine safety, an inde-

pendent report says.... Until legislation is amended... "officials will remain trapped in a confusing and possibly dangerous hiatus where the letter of the law does not accord with expected behaviour".... "The work has suffered. Routine decisions have been delayed because overcautious officials fear criticism." Among some mining companies dealing with the branch, this has resulted in "a disturbing undercurrent of negativity and, in a few cases, outright mistrust." Justice Richard... said the department should no longer have conflicting responsibilities for promoting mineral development, approving mine plans and ensuring "efficient and safe" mining. Mr. Miller says this can be accomplished by abolishing many permits issued by the department. (*Chronicle Herald*, April 18, 1998, A6)

But, unlike conventional suspects who cause harm and death, and are often the subjects of detailed investigative journalism, the press did not probe the backgrounds of the Westray personalities or frame an interpersonal context for their deadly conduct. They registered and re-registered the truth of Westray by highlighting legal maneuvers — the paraphernalia of the big case — and by valorizing criminal justice professionals as authoritative news makers. Typically, legal matters were separated from the site of the production of the event and then rhetorically framed as autonomous. Characters, scenes, actions and events were arranged to exhibit a rather narrow, narrative plot function, the effect of which was to balance law against order.

Thus, judges, defence lawyers, crown prosecutors and inquiry lawyers were the major definers of the news. The police were not prominent sources, except in interval one when they laid out the basis for prosecution. Then citation of them as a source declined dramatically; they were cited in only four news stories after the public inquiry (Table 21).

TABLE 21 — Police Sources and Positions by Time Interval

|  | 1st | 2nd | 3rd |
|---|---|---|---|
| Police Chief and Superintendent | 8 (17.4%) | — | 1 (25.0%) |
| Sergeants and Constables | 22 (47.8%) | 9 (33.3%) | 2 (50.0%) |
| Special Investigators | 4 (8.7%) | 16 (59.3%) | 1 (25.0%) |
| Spokespersons | 9 (19.6%) | 2 (7.4%) | — |
| Unknown | 3 (6.5%) | — | — |
|  | N = 46 | N = 27 | N = 4 |

Legal sources, by contrast, registered trial statements, made requests for legal aid, provided reviews of judicial procedures and advanced legal strategies and debates about the constitutionality of public inquiry proceedings for the press. Even citizens' accounts were embroidered with legal narratives. By the third interval, judges (40 percent) and Crown prosecutors (34 percent) were consistent news makers. In interval three, the Westray Families Group lawyers, government lawyers and civil lawyers were also regularly represented in the news (up from 2 percent to 10 percent; 3 percent to 6 percent; and 2 percent to 5 percent) when compared to interval two. Use of defence lawyers as sources, on the other hand, declined from 15 percent to 5 percent over the same time period (Table 22).

TABLE 22 — Legal Sources and Positions by Time Interval

|  | 1st | 2nd | 3rd |
|---|---|---|---|
| Judges | 56 | 36 | 45 |
|  | (27.9%) | (40.5%) | (40.0%) |
| Crown Prosecutors | 21 | 47 | 38 |
|  | (10.5%) | (14.1%) | (34.0%) |
| Defence Lawyers | 52 | 50 | 6 |
|  | (25.7%) | (14.9%) | (5.4%) |
| Union Lawyers | 11 | 22 | — |
|  | (5.5%) | (6.6%) |  |
| Inquiry Lawyers | 41 | 53 | — |
|  | (20.4%) | (15.8%) |  |
| Westray Families Group Lawyers | 12 | 6 | 11 |
|  | (6.0%) | (1.8%) | (9.8%) |
| Government Lawyers | 8 | 10 | 7 |
|  | (4.0%) | (3.0%) | (6.3%) |
| Civil Lawyers | — | 5 | 5 |
|  |  | (1.5%) | (4.5%) |
| Other | — | 6 | — |
|  |  | (1.8%) |  |
|  | N = 201 | N = 335 | N = 112 |

Compared to legal experts, engineers and mining experts (4 percent, 7 percent, 3 percent), private-sector sources (3 percent, 4 percent, 8 percent) and academic, medical experts and religious authorities (3 percent, 2 percent, 2 percent) were remarkably minor claims makers over all time intervals. Overall the press emphasized the language of "due process" rather than the vocabulary of science or the discourse of criminal culpability. But citizens were consistently represented in the news at about 14 percent of the overall coverage. Of these sources, miners (25 percent, 27 percent, 13 percent), spouses of the deceased (14 percent, 6 percent, 27 percent), other family members (10 percent, 32 percent, 48 percent) and spokespersons for the Westray Families Group (18 percent, 26 percent, 10 percent) communicated most often with the press over the three time intervals (Table 23).

TABLE 23 — Citizen Sources by Time Interval

|  | 1st | 2nd | 3rd |
|---|---|---|---|
| Miners | 56 | 32 | 9 |
|  | (24.4%) | (26.9%) | (13.4%) |
| Victims' Spouses | 33 | 7 | 18 |
|  | (14.3%) | (5.9%) | (26.9%) |
| Victims' Relatives (all types%) | 23 | 38 | 32 |
|  | (10.0%) | (31.9%) | (47.8%) |
| Community Members | 43 | 4 | — |
|  | (18.7%) | (3.3%) |  |
| Draegermen | 17 | 4 | 1 |
|  | (7.4%) | (3.4%) | (1.5%) |
| Westray Families Group | 41 | 31 | 7 |
|  | (17.8%) | (26.1%) | (10.4%) |
| Protest Groups | 17 | 3 | — |
|  | (7.4%) | (2.5%) |  |
|  | N = 230 | N = 119 | N = 67 |

At first these narratives emphasized social psychological language and coded grief, anger and despair as wholly internal. But, by the third interval, the press recast citizen sources to deploy a critique of state and corporate images and accounts about Westray and its aftermath. This critique was bolstered by labour sources who were strategically redeployed in the coverage (up from 2.3 percent in the second reporting interval to 8.2 percent in the third interval). Taken together, as we shall see, these sources helped enact a new regime of truth around political scandal that dramatized the wrongdoings of political heavyweights and public officials without really inculpating senior private economic actors.

> Wayne Cheverie... said as simply and as powerfully as anyone could what this inquiry has to do. "Never again... should workers' lives be risked or deemed expendable for profit".... His story is deeply shocking. A supervisor, he says, set a crucial methane meter to accept higher levels of gas the day before the explosion. Explosive coal dust was ankle deep on the shift before the tragedy, and at times, two feet deep. Welding torches were used underground; safety training was non-existent; work went on in gas concentrations three times the level for mandatory evacuation. The responses of mine officials to complaints about safety were reprimand and intimidation.... A mine inspector told him — wrongly — he had no power to shut down the mine for safety

violations. Mr. Cheverie's observations are horribly consistent with expert testimony.... It seems failures by many people went into the making of this tragedy. But a bleak overall picture is emerging of workplace safety standards appropriate to the Dark Ages... we need a system that guarantees inspectors professional independence from political pressure, real or perceived. This would give workers more confidence to defy browbeating bosses and report hazards. Wayne Cheverie's story is like a harsh and painful light in the eyes. It should be used to lead us out of very deadly Dark Ages. (*Chronicle Herald*, January 20, 1996, C3)

The judge also absolved the miners both dead and living, of blame. While some had "undoubtedly indulged in many dangerous and foolhardy practices, he said intimidation of workers and managements emphasis on production led to tampering with methane detectors and other improper acts. "Had it not been for these unsafe practices attributed to the miners, would the explosion of May 9th occurred?" he asked in the report. "The answer must be yes it would have." (*Chronicle Herald*, December 2, 1997, A1)

But overall, subversive accounts emanating from citizens, local protest groups, draegermen, unions and other mining federations were minor representations in the total news coverage.

At bottom, the press followed official sources in making the news. They enacted an ideological formation of natural disaster without embedding it in a political economy framework. They mobilized a discourse of legal tragedy rather than one of law and order. They developed a critical discourse about political malfeasance, but diverted public attention away from the world of private capital and the corporation. How can we account for the media's politics of truth and truth transformation? Did changes in news sources and claims making assemble new "regimes of truth" about Westray? Why was Westray represented as a crime that never happened? How does the media representation of Westray compare with other studies of the media and corporate violence?

## Note

1    As mentioned in the previous chapter, the three time intervals were: interval one — February 9, 1992, to December 31, 1994; interval two — January 1, 1995, to December 31, 1997; and interval three — January 1, 1998, to August 9, 2002.

# 6. The Politics of Truth and The Invisibility of Corporate Crime

## The Transformation of Truth: From Disaster to Tragedy

Over time, the quantity and quality of news coverage changed: what could and could not be said, by whom and in what language, shifted. The news reporting in the first time interval reflected the volatility and chaos of the explosion. In the immediate aftermath, Curragh Resources policed the territorial site for the production of truth. They enacted power by controlling context. Reporters were denied entry to the mine site; employers and their families were instructed to stay away from the press, because the "media lied" (Jobb 1994: 59). Curragh officials, in turn, informed the press that worried families did not want to speak to them. On the outside of the information barricade, the press waited and reacted to the information flow and to the deadlines set by Curragh Resources. As one reporter observed "We were feeding off each other... waiting for their briefings... there was no real news, they just felt that they had to come, and we felt that we had to write or broadcast something" (cited in Richards 1999: 152). Corporate spokespersons tied reporters to their version of veracity by providing diagrams, maps and photographs; arranging press hearings at company convenience, so that stories could be filed without reaction from others; and channelling information into technical plot lines that empowered corporate advisors as authoritative claims makers (McMullan and Hinze 1999). They took advantage of the reporters' lack of time, informants and routines to create their own news sources, attempting to create a "best news" story in the context of a "bad news" crisis. News was strategically produced so as to proactively engender publicity that created overall confidence in corporate behaviour. It was primarily a "communication between journalists and their preferred corporate sources, with the remainder of the public left in the position of spectator" (Ericson et al. 1989: 260). As van Dijk (1993: 260) notes, in this type of situation some "voices are thereby censored, some opinions are not heard, some perspectives are ignored: the discourse itself becomes a segregated structure." Or, as one miner involved in the rescue effort put it, "I have never seen so much snow in May. The media was snowed and so was everyone else." The company, he insists, controlled "every bit of information given out to the public and the families" (Comish 1993: 48).

The corporate control of information was sometimes insensitive to the concerns of the families. One woman reported how she heard the news of her husband's death:

> He [mine manager] walked in the fire hall and got his coffee first. He put his hand through his hair, and walked down to the front dry-eyed as can be. I passed out when I heard, just for a moment, but I came to and they [Curragh officials] didn't even come to see if I was okay. And I was not that far away from them. (Cited in Richards 1999: 153)

Others complained about "truth" issues. Curragh often informed the media first and then told the families something different later. As one family member recalled:

> I'd leave the fire hall and go to the hotel for the night, and watch television.... It'd be a totally different story from what they told us. It was a more complete story. I'd rather myself know than the country. (Cited in Richards 1999: 153)

As some families spent hours waiting to identify their dead, they grew suspicious, thinking that the delays were related to corporate politics:

> [Father-in-law]: our [son-in-law's] body was one of the first recovered... we decided almost immediately that we wanted a complete autopsy.... [mother-in-law]: we were told that we would be able to see his body at seven o'clock in the evening. We left the fire hall at about two in the afternoon. We got word... to be at the basement of the church at seven [p.m.] but we didn't see his body until, what, six in the morning?... it bothered me that officials, if you will, were taking this long to prepare a body before we would see it. (Cited in Dodd 1999: 230–31)

The Emergency Measures Coordinator himself complained that the mine operator was lax in providing reliable and timely information to the waiting families. Company briefings were technical, presented by an accountant who could not answer many of the families' questions. This contributed to a tense atmosphere in the fire hall, and the problems did not end there. When the families were about to issue a press release on May 14th to thank their supporters and friends, they were pre-empted by Curragh Resources's announcement that the rescue-recovery operation was discontinued. Some emergency services had not been informed of this decision; they now had to comfort a newly shocked population who were shattered by the impact of sudden bereavement (Smith nd.: 3).

The truth of Westray, furthermore, was being denied even as the bodies of the dead were being reclaimed from the mine. Before the rescue efforts commenced, advance plans for "maximum deniability" began along with documented instructions about what to lie about. Curragh Incorporated hired the services of a public relations firm, Reid Management, to immediately manufacture and manage impressions surrounding the explosion. Reid faxed instructions to Curragh's operations director telling him to advise the media of the following:

> This is a terrible human tragedy that could not be foreseen. The company has done everything physically and humanly possible to guard against dangerous conditions.... There have been no dangerous or suspicious conditions or methane gas readings: dust kept under strict control. There were no warnings of any kind. Safety always the first consideration. Dangers acknowledged daily.... mine designed for safety and emergencies.... Procedures carefully monitored.... The families, rescue teams and other employees have demonstrated extraordinary courage.... The company will encourage a comprehensive examination of the causes of the accident to ensure against similar tragedies in the future. (Cited in Cameron et al. 1994: 56)

This nihilation strategy emphasized what Arendt (1995: 84–86) calls "language rules": on one track, the language was compassionate and caring, on the other, there were guidelines on how to disguise reality by cover-up and euphemism. The victims of Westray were "courageous" workers, employed at a mine where "everything physically and humanly possible to guard against dangerous conditions" had been in place and where there had been "no warnings of any kind." This public discourse was highly coded, full of sanctimonious references to hope, fortitude, dying hard and the desire of the company to examine the "causes of the accident" to prevent "similar tragedies in the future." These narratives addressed certain social anxieties in their reading and listening audiences. They achieved prevalence by offering courage as a kind of consolation in the face of a world which, they also asserted, was dangerous and difficult to comprehend. Because such "tragic-natural-accident" accounts permeated peoples lives as consumers of the news so persistently and so intimately, the institutional and discursive sites of their production were often lost or forgotten (Kellner 1990). In this way, corporate capital both disavowed the meaning of Westray and claimed they did not understand it. The simultaneity of literal denial and discursive justification was essential for later official news production, for Curragh's legal strategy and for the construction of a news audience. As Goff (2001: 203) observes:

> This massive coverage in the immediate aftermath provided smothering detail of the tragedy: the explosion, the attempt to rescue the trapped miners, discovering the bodies, flooding the mine and the suffering of the families. It was the human interest

story next door, a tragedy in a primary industry in a traditional economy. However, much of the reporting is not critical or informative, but emotional... [and] full of sentimental phrases.

These strategies allowed Curragh to circulate their "truth" about the explosion through public relations ritual and rhetoric. They wrote the central scripts, provided the stage and counselled their actors for a pop-culture drama, while reporters were left to write about the performance. The press was encouraged not to question the role of private capital in the disaster. In Jobb's words, the media emphasized "the trivial," "the fluff and feelies," "the peoples angles" and "the human interest" (cited in Richards 1999: 156).

The assembly of this "regime of truth" ran contrary to the most obvious fact scenario: that is, maintaining it required both effort and blindness. The Westray story contained evidence of questionable mining practices, including the long history of mining deaths in the region, Curragh Resources' troubled safety record in Canada, public reservations from capital and labour about mining the coal seam and problems associated with the methods used in the mine. In addition, the widespread political involvement in brokering the mine into existence, including guaranteed loans, subsidies, tax incentives, infrastructure grants and protected coal markets at inflated prices were well known, as was public information regarding government reluctance to take action against occupational health and safety violations at the mine (Glasbeek 2003; Glasbeek and Tucker 1999; Tucker 1995; Hynes and Prasad 1999). The press may have continuously reported the explosion as a human interest story because they had failed to critically investigate Westray previously. The media ignored complaint stories. They did not think that critics had credibility. The press would roll their eyes when opposition MLAs spoke of safety issues at the mine site. When the explosion occurred, reporters were reluctant to pick up a story they had previously minimized as unimportant. As Richards (1999: 159) notes:

> Journalists were caught in the position of trying to explain an event that they did not understand. The effort required to do so meant that the crisis was compartmentalized, as if separate from the wider context of technology and Canada's reliance on coal as a resource, which make such events both predictable and inevitable.

Although to some extent this was true, the press did eventually develop a political economy discourse of the explosion that provided a wider context. The news was not without critical perspective in the early representation of Westray. About one-quarter of the news narratives did trace connections between high unemployment and risky capital ventures in the region. Within weeks of the explosion, journalists signified the promise of a socio-economic explanation for the disaster. But corporate and state officials were adroit at restricting this news discourse. As one miner put it:

> The company was very good at deception.... I knew something was going on as soon as I saw the pretty boy they had brought in from Toronto to do all the T.V. reports.... He did an excellent job of making the public feel sorry for the company, but it was all done that way with one goal in mind: public pity. (Comish 1993: 47)

By deflecting blame and stressing "interpretive denial," the company emphasized what van Dijk (1998: 61) terms "positive self-presentation and negative other-presentation." The mine blew up on its own! In other words, "what happened was really something else" — a natural accident. "The gas is to blame for the explosion which rocked the Westray mine... and claimed the lives of at least 11 miners.... If methane's explosive properties are not the cause of death, then its qualities as a toxic gas can kill a miner trapped in a damaged mine shaft" (*Chronicle Herald*, May 11, 1992: A2). This was the politics of truth that defined "the limits and the forms of the sayable" about Westray; the press enacted and conferred considerable legitimacy on this "regime of truth" both in the early reporting interval and throughout the decade of coverage (Foucault 1980b, 1991b).

The press focused on the sorrow, sacrifice and suffering inherent in managing sudden death. Journalists evoked strong emotive images and symbols about how families, friends and rescuers coped with the despair and the discovery of dead bodies: "I told the families never to give up hope," "death was quiet and painless," "exhausted dragger men cried... they returned to their motel emotionally wrung out" (*Chronicle Herald*, May 13, 1992: A1; May 15, 1992: B3, A2). A mining disaster was reworked as a familial trauma where the actual explosion — its causes, agents and harms — were written to the margins of the news texts. The effect of this reporting was to distance the corporation from the event.

> The families feel no anger toward the mining company... except a desire to get this over with. (*Chronicle Herald*, May 12, 1992: A15

> I will go back despite the tragedy.... Westray followed safety guidelines; if they hadn't, we would have complained. (*Chronicle Herald*, May 11, 1992: A14

> Now they are torn: should they return to the same mine that exploded three weeks ago, look for another job or quit mining forever? (*Chronicle Herald*, May 30, 1992: A2)

In turn, these versions of events initiated "literal denial" of both corporate and individual culpability ("nothing illegal happened"), and empowered and enabled the media's "evasion of responsibility" in portraying both interpretive and literal denial as fact. As McCormick (1995: 208) notes, "the politics of the disaster received little attention" or was contextualized in benign terms: "A somber expression that told the story of good intentions gone wrong." If he could have predicted what happened, the Premier is quoted as saying, "I'm sure we would have made different judgments" (*Chronicle Herald*, May 23, 1992: C1). The portrayal of the disaster is one in which the explosion was unpredictable and politicians were uninvolved in its making. As Goff (2001: 210) rightly observes, the press "refused to call the explosion a 'homicide' and rarely if ever followed up on this issue with any investigative reports." So media denial was neither a matter of telling the truth nor of intentionally telling a lie; it was a matter of "blocking out." The press both knew and didn't know at the same time (Cohen 2001: 113–16).

The natural tragedy discourse declined substantially by 1995; evidence of corporate wrongdoing and state negligence arising out of the regulatory and police investigations and the criminal trial led to a discursive reformulation that displaced political economy narratives in the news coverage. The "conditions for possible statements" were altered as new claims makers emerged to construct "new forms of positivity" about Westray (Foucault 1991b: 69). The previous "politics of truth" was destabilized by gaps, inconsistencies, discontinuities and disbelief in the information of once accredited official sources. Cartoons, for example, captured the subversive realignment in press reporting. Their numbers nearly doubled in the second reporting period and their images conveyed the parodic. One portrayed a picture of six newspapers in separate frames under the headlines:

> "Lack of safety at Westray Astonishing!" — Worker; "Westray Worst Mine I Ever Saw" — Expert; "Westray Sets Record for World's Crappiest Mine" — Guinness Book of World Records; "Westray Really, Really Sucked Bad" — Electrician; "Westray Gross, Yuck, Ptooey!!" — Just About Everybody; "Pattern Developing in Westray Testimony." (*Chronicle Herald*, January 25, 1996, B1)

A second characterized a labour official as "Mine Inspector Clouseau." The caption read: "Everything looked fine to me, although it was hard to tell with all that coal dust everywhere" (*Chronicle Herald*, May 9, B1). Another lampooned the public inquiry report. It showed a sketch of the Westray Report leaning against a gravestone under the heading "Cold Comfort" (*Chronicle Herald*, December 2, 1997, C1). "Truth" was contested and reworked in the news to speak to power in a language of "legal tragedy."

Yet this new "politics of truth" did not typically demarcate procedural law from substantive law, or highlight the social context or the criminal content of the case against the Westray accused. Rather, truth telling was mostly self-referential and abstract. It registered routine stories about professional conduct, the presentation of evidence, legal proceedings and judicial decision-making. Criminal trial coverage, for example, chronicled events in a restricted, mundane manner. Each news report was a relatively autonomous narrative. Typically, it almost always began with statements such as "in today's proceedings," or "today the court passed a ruling that" and concluded with statements such as "tomorrow the court will resume with...."

News-truth was a faithful catalogue of procedural correctness, competing versions of culpability, scientific witnessing and blame-smithing. It followed the premise that legal procedure was the means through which the truth of Westray would be uncovered, even if that truth muddied the boundary between accident and negligent or willful misconduct. Yet, at the same time, the legal discourse, with its emphasis on documents, testimony, hired counsels, examinations, credentials, cross-examinations and exhibits, expanded the scope of the sayable. It opened up spaces for additional truth claims to come forward from medical, police and scientific sources, even though the assumptions, vocabularies and reasonings of the legal form provided the ultimate filter regarding blame, motives and causality. The press coverage of the criminal trial and its legal aftermath represented a "discursive threshold" where "the rules governing the production and dissemination of truth statements" about Westray recast a natural event with a tragic subject into a legal tragedy with a non-culpable subject (Foucault 1990: 94). This discursive shift was one element in a broader discursive transformation that crystallized around the public inquiry (Foucault 1991b). Here the boundaries of the permissible concerning statements of truth about Westray were further expanded: conflicting narratives empowered by heterogeneous voices were registered in an official public forum and reported on by the press. While the adversarial rules and procedures governing statements of truth in the criminal trial worked to conceal narratives of intent, blame and censure, the revelations at the public inquiry prised open new mechanisms of truth discovery and validation. In Foucault's (1990a: 112) words, it hastened a transformation which did not correspond "to the calm, continuist image" that is normally accredited to regimes of truth associated with natural disaster or legal tragedy.

## The Representation of Scandal and the Disqualification
of Crime as Truth

The public inquiry, however, did not encourage the press to tell the truth about Westray as a crime, even though crime news is a primary genre of media reporting (Ericson et al. 1991; Chermak 1994; Barak 1994; Surrette 1998). By their nature, public inquiries are official responses to controversial cases. They are surrounded by vocabularies of responsibility and liability. Conducted by senior judges and serviced by networks of legal and technical experts, inquiries are linked to the apportionment of blame. Interested parties hire lawyers to safeguard their interests and, where needed, to deflect liability. Unfortunately those most affected by a tragic event have little input into the priorities and focuses of an inquiry. The government determines the shape and scope of the inquiry, which often reflects its preferred view of what happened. More positively, inquiry recommendations do carry the weight of a costly and indepth investigation, which has drawn on a mass of unsolicited as well as requested opinion and evidence. Findings are derived by meticulous rituals of cross-examination conducted by lawyers representing the interests of all major parties with standing. Seen as objective, but commissioned by the state, the presumption is that the inquiry can uncover the truth, provide a systemic understanding of context and mobilize solutions that will be respected (Tucker 1995).

The discursive boundaries governing what could and could not be said at the Westray inquiry, however, were drawn to delineate political misconduct from corporate criminal wrongdoing. The rules governing media accusations were embedded in relations of power and authority. When Westray was registered in a law-and-order discourse, the press typically attributed a criminal status to middle managers in corporate and governmental institutions. Senior corporate and governmental officials, who set the codes governing decision-making and directed the regulation of subordinates, were usually ascribed a politically undeserving status. The former deserved demotions, dismissals or criminal sanctions; the latter were "misfits" in need of manners, morals and improvement.

The public inquiry operated as a ceremony of power, where the press produced political drama. They narrated hearing conduct, reported witness testimony and evaluated public figures. The inquiry's truth mechanism approximated a disciplinary apparatus. In Foucault's (1995: 181) words, the inquiry "hierarchized the 'good' and the 'bad' subjects in relation to one another" and judged them "in truth." Reporters, for their part, discursively ranked and graded business executives, politicians, experts, inspectors and miners. Press classifications and comparisons identified notable individuals and linked them to dubious blameworthy political and regulatory behaviour. This examination process punished and rewarded; it combined "the penal functioning of setting in order and the ordinal character of judging" (Foucault 1995: 181).

The media's "politics of truth" acknowledged some harm about those who died, but rarely the larger victimization: the hundreds of disrupted lives and the demoralization associated with job loss were seldom recorded in the news. For example, the civil suit by the bereaved families encouraged reporting that discovered "official mistakes," but the reports usually omitted a vocabulary of negligence. Similarly reporters rarely inquired into the public inquiry proper, asking questions such as who are the commissioners? What values and assumptions do they hold and how similar are they to those held by corporate and government officials? To what degree can legal processes shape acceptable reforms? How just can this process be to the dead and to their living relatives and friends? The press interpolated a guarded acknowledgement of accountability about Westray. While they opened up questions about legal truths and truth tellers, they often disqualified discussions about legal culpability and downplayed the discourse of structured corporate violence. Consider the following news items:

> Prosecutors should reconsider pursuing criminal charges against two former mine officials in light of the findings of the inquiry into the Westray disaster, a defence lawyer says. Gordon Kelly says Justice Richard's sweeping condemnation of the coal mine's management and government safety inspectors raises questions about why an rcmp investigation singled out top managers Gerald Phillips and Roger Parry. "With the blame that he spreads around, you've got to ask yourself why anybody's charged," Mr. Kelly says. "There were a lot of people who were involved in running this mine, top to bottom," Kevin Coady said. "You can't just go and grab two people and say 'let's hammer these guys.'" Mr. Kelly feels the report largely attacks Mr. Phillips' character and management style. "The issue (in the criminal case) isn't whether he's a good guy or a bad guy. The issue is whether he did what they say he did." (*Chronicle Herald*, December 3, 1997, A3)

> Mr. Downe also did something no other member of government has done in the five and a half years since the explosion. Choosing his words carefully, he apologized for "any role the government may have played" in the disaster. "We are deeply sorry for the Westray disaster." (*Chronicle Herald*, December 19, 1997, A1)

Of course, as the judicial aftermath unfolded, journalists and editors were more inclined to narrate the need for social justice. But responsibility and resolution were not really registered in the news until Justice Richard valorized them in his official public commission. Nevertheless media "truth finding" and "truth telling" acknowledged the disaster in a language that challenged corporate and state-sanctioned regimes of truth, and inscribed further "modifications in the rules of the formation of statements" that were accepted as truth and truthful (Foucault 1980a: 112).

Legal narratives operated intradiscursively with a vocabulary of political approbation to place some blame, however hesitantly, in the corridors of power. Despite a downturn in the sheer volume of legal, law-and-order, and political and regulatory failure narratives, the tone of the news became more critical of the powerful. Part of the explanation for this discursive shift was the willingness of the press to eventually consider subaltern voices — bereaved family members, miners and union representatives — more favourably and to redeploy and reregister their stories as truth narratives. Another part of the explanation was the discursive support provided by legal and scientific experts, who opened up "innumerable points of confrontation and at least temporarily inverted power relations" (Foucault 1995: 27). Legal sources functioned as truth tellers on two interrelated discursive fronts. The press mobilized them to explicate how the public inquiry functioned as a radical mechanism of "truth discovery," and to act as truth-sayers positing new claims about corporate and government misconduct and violence. Legal experts guided the flow of information, exposed contradictions in witnesses' statements, countered vague and ambiguous corporate and government answers with additional background information and precise follow-ups, and constructed complete truths from half-truths. The press accredited these experts and, to a large degree, produced the truth of their power. Consider the subversive tone of lawyers' talk later in the news reports:

> There's a problem with the regulator in this province. It isn't that they made a mistake. It's that they refused to acknowledge that they made a mistake. And that strikes me as being a very serious problem.... You've just given me a long answer trying to justify your actions... refusing to acknowledge that anything went off the rails — and that's the problem. (*Chronicle Herald*, May 3, 1996, A3)

> Sir, you want the commission and the rest of the people in this room to believe... that they're all lying and only you, Albert McLean, is telling the truth? (*Chronicle Herald*, May 14, 1996, A6)

> Mr. Merrick reviewed the circumstances of Mr. Guptill's complaints and his later firing, and suggested there may have been a behind-the-scenes plan: "A Mr. Guptill comes forward with a range of complaints, including an injury. I'm going to suggest to

you that the evidence may support the conclusion that Mr. Phillips puts on his charming hat and a cheque, apologizes to Mr. Guptill, takes statements from all the men involved and in effect sort of buys a solution to the complaint until the department has closed its file. Then they threaten to put Guptill underground again, so he has to quit. So, the net result of all this is that a man who had safety complaints and an injury gets bought off by the company until the inspectorate has closed their files — and then, in effect, gets forced out." (*Chronicle Herald*, May 16, 1996, A1)

Justice Richard said he has been left with the impression the province's internal responsibility system provides a very neat vehicle for the inspectorate to dodge their responsibilities. (*Chronicle Herald*, June, 12, 1996, A1)

Scientific experts added to this process of reframing. While less numerous in the coverage, the press redeployed engineers', geologists' and surveyors' accounts at the public inquiry to re-explain the immediate causes of the explosion, to re-evaluate the viability of the mining enterprise and the vigilance of the safety inspectorate, and to redetermine whether the explosion could have been prevented. These accounts at the inquiry were strategically reregistered by the press as both political and moral objections to local, corporate and political officialdom.

Things went wrong at the Westray mine not because of "an act of God — it was just misplanning," a Colorado mining engineer said…. the Provincial Labour and Natural Resources departments both had responsibilities, that, at times, neither carried out… so it is not giving you the impression of a very thorough, competent enforcement. (*Chronicle Herald*, January 19, 1996, A3)

The report by Andrew Linley, a mine ventilation export from England was released at the provincial inquiry…. Mr. Phillips didn't have the qualifications to be a mining engineer as he claimed…. Mr. Linley describes John Vincent Smith, an electrical and mechanical inspector, as being uninterested in his job, incompetent or both. Mr. Smith's lack of awareness of events at Westray (suggests he gave the Westray management on unduly easy ride and failed to ensure regulations were upheld…. "You can't sit back and assume or presume that everything's going to be done right." (*Chronicle Herald*, January 16, 1996, A3)

In contrast to the reporting of the "emergency" phase of the explosion, corporate and state officials were unable to sustain what Cohen

(1993, 1996, 2001) and Arendt (1971, 1972, 1995) call "literal forms of denial" e.g., what happened was a tragic accident! Mendacity could no longer contain the awful truth of the explosion. As Cohen (2001: 106) observes,

> If literal denial is countered by irrefutable evidence that something indeed happened: the strategy may switch to legalistic reinterpretations or political justifications.... There is room for legitimate controversy, claims and counter-claims, not because of the socio-legal truism that all actions are interpreted, but because the dominant language of interpretation is legal.

The "politics of definition," especially at the inquiry, forced regulators, corporate actors and politicians to enact new "games of truth." "Interpretative denial" enabled state and corporate actors to admit the raw facts but deny the framework placed on them. This functioned in the news to mystify the boundary between rhetoric and referent in regard to responsibility and culpability. The following editorial provides a good example of this process:

> Buchanan's message was clear: Any Westray proposals put before cabinet were the responsibility not of Buchanan, but of premier-to-be Cameron.... "Before 1990, I was the premier of Nova Scotia." This was the senator's quaint way of saying he didn't know much about what happened at Westray after he went to... the Canadian senate. Buchanan's rambling testimony had one thing in common with Cameron's.... Both men, in common with the score of government witnesses who went before them, refused to take any blame for the tragedy that killed 26 men on May 9th, 1992. (*Chronicle Herald*, May 31, 1996, C1)

Some corporate officials and politicians attempted to exonerate themselves by deploying tactics of "implicatory denial" and "condemnation of condemners." They attacked the credibility of victims ("the miners are lying"), accused the inquiry of being biased against them ("they just want to blame someone so they are blaming me"), or excused their actions through appeals to higher righteousness ("we had to cut corners in order to meet production quotas"). Consider the Premier's and former Premier's testimonies:

> The mine blew up because of "what happened that morning" and not because of any political pressure from the province. "I don't understand why people don't come back and take responsibility," he said, referring to miners who allegedly doctored methane

> monitors and ignored safety problems underground. (*Chronicle Herald*, May 29, 1996, C1)

> His [Buchanan's] testimony differed from Cameron's in tone, and in its insistence that Donnie himself was largely responsible for the Westray file.... [Cameron's] comments before the Westray inquiry, blaming miners for the tragedy and federal bureaucrats for its prelude, were more outrageous in tone than they were in content.... his view that ministers and premiers are not responsible for the actions of the public service dismisses any notion of accountable government.... [MacKay] is the former federal cabinet minister who somehow managed to escape the inquiry without adequately explaining how an... indifferent Prime Minister by the name of Mulroney allowed his cabinet to approve an $80 million loan guarantee for Curragh... it's been a week of dodging at the Westray inquiry — some of it artful, some of it a donnybrook. (*Chronicle Herald*, May 31, 1996, C1)

These forms of official denial were made possible by the privileged positions enjoyed by the corporation in the local economy and by the intervention of government institutions in the process of truth discovery, investigation, inquiry and adjudication. Both tried to exploit negative attitudes and behaviours on the part of workers, in the mine and in the community, in their process of condemnation. Curragh's manipulations of the truth, the rescinding of regulatory charges, lax police investigation practices, the collapse of the public prosecution, flawed criminal justice procedures, paltry compensation payments, spurious allegations in the press and failure to discipline those responsible and compensate those victimized, all contributed to the "demonization" of the dead and their families. Marginalized as "other," that is, other than deserving, honest and reasonable, the bereaved at once experienced dissociation and dehumanization (Dodd 1999; Davis 2003). The wife of a deceased miner put it as follows:

> There's no justice in all this. Like Clifford Frame said in the paper the other day, "It was a simple accident." Well come on, you're sitting up there in Toronto with a cigar in your mouth, you know. Let it be one of your sons and say, "Oh it was just a simple accident." Oh that really hurts. (Cited in Dodd 1999: 241)

The mother of another dead miner remarked:

> There are 26 of them. You know my son didn't want to die down there. So why? Why should they be doing what they're doing to

us? And why isn't this solved? And why don't they punish the ones that did this? (Cited in Dodd 1999: 242)

A brother describes the cruel legacy of the failure of the criminal trial and the public inquiry.

> Frame and that Pelley, I mean, if they're not trying to hide nothing why couldn't they come down, do their thing, get it all over with now, you know? Let us get on with our lives. Lord Jesus we'll be dead before it's over. I get all these things all balled up inside me.... My nerves go on me and I get so stressed. I just feel that everything's falling down on me. (Cited in Dodd 1999: 244)

Corporate officials, who once controlled the production of news, also resorted to "passive denial"; they closed their shells and took "potshots" from afar. To protect their interests, when their versions of veracity were being disbelieved, they signalled the absence of a problem. As Cohen (2001: 102–103) observes: "because of pressures from outside (stigmatization, sanctions, boycotts, isolation) and their own internal ideology (everyone is against us, no one understands us), [the powerful] see no political necessity for dialogue with the rest of the world."

Curragh Resources' senior executives and mine managers condemned the public inquiry calling it a "railroad job and a farce" (*Chronicle Herald*, April 18, 1996, A1). As their CEO put it, "they just want to label me... they're probably not even interested in what I have to say" (*Chronicle Herald*, September 6, 1997). Corporate officials encouraged a language and belief that denied the morality of their own behaviour. Unable to accept any legitimate universe outside their own they had no need to claim to be innocent of troubling recognitions of wrongdoings because those recognitions were not troubling to them at all.

> Westray miners have described walking through thick drifts of dust, but Frame believes the dust contained enough impurities to make it safe.... All this leaves Frame with a clear conscience. "Christ, I'm sitting up here in Toronto.... How in the name of God would I know that anyone was adjusting a methane detector? How the hell would I know that? And if I didn't know that, how could I have any feeling of guilt, other than the fact that I shouldn't have developed the God damned mine in the first place." (*Chronicle Herald*, November 11, 1997, A12)

> [Phillips] challenged the grim portrayal of the way the mine operated under his command. "It's simple to blame someone. The simplest person to blame is me".... At the inquiry, miners and

> foremen have testified that pressure from senior management —
> Phillips included — forced workers to cut corners and take risks.
> Phillips, however, contends he was not aware employees were
> breaking the law. (*Chronicle Herald*, May 19, 1966, A5)

The central issues of corporate responsibility and liability, workplace
safety, and the duty of caring for the lives of those underground were
deflected and minimized by a discourse coded with legal legerdemain:
"what really happened" was not homicide, but careless, preventable mistakes and bad judgments that cannot be legally satisfied. Workplace violence was cognitively redefined and reallocated to a different, less censori-
ous order. Indeed corporate capital refused to testify at the public inquiry,
and this evasion of the truth-telling process further diminished their
credibility as news makers.

> Where's Cliff Frame when you really need him? Well, the former
> boss of the Westray mine will have to duck (or should we say
> stoop) a little lower now if he wants to avoid the long, slow-
> moving arm of the Westray inquiry.... So won't you come home,
> Cliff? The best way to regain some credibility in mining circles
> may well be making a full and frank disclosure to the people of
> Nova Scotia — on behalf of those 26 men who died so tragically
> on May 9th, 1992. (*Chronicle Herald*, February 5, 1997, C1)

> Mr. Frame and Mr. Pelley do have every legal right to oppose
> subpoenas. But if they did what is right, these legal instruments
> would be unnecessary. And what is right is very simple: they
> should co-operate with the inquiry.... For the two executives to
> refuse to participate in a legitimate public inquiry is outrageous
> and shameful.... The right and honorable thing for them to do is
> to answer, without subpoenas. (*Chronicle Herald*, 1996, July 30, C1)

> By attacking the integrity of the inquiry, by attacking the truth-
> fulness of our members and other witnesses, Phillips has surren-
> dered any claim he might have to special consideration.... It's
> intolerable that he should be making these attacks without the
> inquiry doing whatever it can to bring him forward as a wit-
> ness.... Mr. Phillips has lost any right to hide behind the criminal
> charges.... If he has evidence he has a duty... to bring that
> forward.... They have a moral obligation to assist this inquiry.
> (*Chronicle Herald*, 1996, April 29, A3).

Similarly, government officials' and politicians' claims and counter
claims were reported with incredulity.

Mr. McLean often tried to deflect responsibility from himself onto supervisors or mine managers. (*Chronicle Herald*, April 9, 1996, A1)

What we heard was a denial of any responsibility for failures to spot or correct safety violations before the tragedy, and a litany of sometimes incredible excuses that provoked groans from victims' relatives. (*Chronicle Herald*, 1996, April 10, B1)

Both men [John Buchanan and Donald Cameron], in common with the score of government witnesses who went before them, refused to take any blame for the tragedy.... It's been a week of artful dodging at the inquiry. (*Chronicle Herald*, May 31, 1996, C1)

Senior lawyer John Merrick lashed out at bureaucratic dodging of responsibility for the blast.... "There is a problem with the regulator in this province. It isn't that they made a mistake. It's that they refused to acknowledge that they made a mistake. And that strikes me as a very serious problem." (*Chronicle Herald*, April 3, 1996, A3)

By contrast, the sworn testimony of miners, citizens and experts was increasingly coded as more believable by the media. The press chronicled webs of official denial and deceit. They mobilized a myriad of moral signifiers to reframe the explosion and its legal aftermath. It was "an abuse of authority," "government corruption," "managerial indifference," "bureaucratic bungling," "failure of duty," "safety lapses" and "incompetence." The reporting of Westray as spectacularly tragic and a legal tragedy without a culpable subject was joined by a coverage that traversed and contested these truth-telling narratives. The reactive reporting of the emergency phase and the criminal trial process was eclipsed by a more multidimensional coverage that problematized previous "truth games" and the grip it had on them. Truth flowed upwards "from below" and statements clustered around a signification of "political bankruptcy" as another regime of Westray's truth.

[the miners] have asked cabinet to settle up now, rather than delaying until assets are sold. Given the circumstances of Westray — a disaster that was in large part of government making — that was a reasonable request. Many Westray families are still trying to overcome the financial consequences of a disaster that government negligence allowed to happen. Here, then, was a ready opportunity for the . . . government to demonstrate both humanity and a real sense of accountability. Instead, it has scurried behind the skirts of its lawyers' gowns.... The message is [that] taking responsibility, in our political culture, remains an assignment for government speechwriters. It is not to be confused with paying actual damages to people injured by government.... "All help short of relief" might have been coined for cabinets' approach to Westray victims. And "sorry is as sorry does" is the test it [the government] has flunked. Even partial payment of the severance would have been a show of good faith. That cabinet could not even do this much is disgraceful. Forty-three days ago, we said the Westray report cried out for "a serious reassessment of the meaning of public responsibility." Like the miners, we're still waiting. (*Chronicle Herald*, January 1, 1998, B1)

## Westray, The Press and Corporate Crime

When the press coverage of Westray is compared to other studies of corporate crime and the media, we discover similarities and differences. While there has been a tremendous growth in the number of studies exploring the media's representation of crime in a variety of formats (Barak 1994, 1997; Bailey and Hale 1998; Chermak 1994, 1995; Roberts and Doob 1990; Sacco 1995; Ericson et al. 1987; Surrette 1998), overwhelmingly these studies have focused on street crime and excluded the treatment of serious events such as business crime. For example, Lynch, Stretesky and Hammond (2000: 121–24), in their study of chemical crimes in the U.S. found that newspapers did not report such events because they did not fit the public's image of crime. Similarly, in the media coverage of the Imperial Foods Products fire, which claimed the lives of twenty-six workers and injured fifty-six others, Wright et al. (1995) discovered that the press reluctantly reported the criminality of the event, and when they did, it was the least extensive and least prominently placed coverage in the newspapers. Evans and Lundman (1983), in their study of the print media and the heavy electrical equipment antitrust cases, also found that the reporting was notable for its absence. They concluded that "newspaper journalists" were "not accustomed to viewing corporations as capable of criminality" (1983: 538).

Westray, however, was not "excluded" or "buried" news (Randall et al. 1988: 292), and the reporting of it confirms Levi's (1987: 11) observation that downplaying white-collar disasters in the media may be an "oversimplification." Westray was dramatized to form interesting reading, even though it was not a financial crime and even though it was based upon acts of omission: not testing for methane and coal dust levels, not acting upon information about management violations, not meeting standards of maintenance in the mine, not training inspectors to do their jobs properly and not responding to regulatory warnings, appeals and threats. It has been fictionalized on radio and stage and memorialized in a celebrated television documentary available from national video distributors. The reporting of Westray confirms the wisdom of the observation of Slapper and Tombs (1999: 92), that "there are no real reasons why dramatized accounts of corporate offending need be any less (or more) interesting than those of conventional crimes."

Second, the reporting of Westray contradicts findings that say journalists are homogeneous in their reporting of corporate crime (Lofquist 1997; Wright et al. 1995; Lynch et al. 1989; McCormick 1995; Molotch and Lester 1978). The news-making process around Westray was neither static nor predictable. The production of news truth was certainly informed by a "dominant news frame," but news representations were also discontinous constructions. In Dean's (1994: 47) words, images and representations were "techniques of power" and were "the very material form of power itself." This was evident in the several interpretations that made up Westray's truth, in the press's reflexive use of different news sources and in the struggles over social meanings found in different genres of storywriting (i.e., cartoons, editorials, news reports). At bottom, Westray instructs us that the media coverage of corporate disasters can be dynamic and can change in volume, form and content, especially when indictments, prosecutions and public inquiries are involved (Swigert and Farell 1980; Lynch, Nalla and Miller 1989; Evans, Cullen and Dubeck 1993).

Third, the news coverage of Westray did produce a prominent-accident or natural-tragedy "regime of truth," but, despite considerable efforts by corporate and government spokespersons, it was not always dominant in the news reporting. The Westray explosion presented new developments over the course of the decade, and new events generated more news, which, in turn, challenged the accident discourse. The reporting of Westray contrasts with Molotch and Lester's (1978), Evans and Lundman's (1983), Wright et al.'s (1995), Lofquist's (1997), Slapper and Tombs' (1999) and Lynch, Stretesky and Hammond's (2000) research that found that the "language of accidents" (discrete, isolated, random, intentional acts conveying the unforeseeable, unknowable and unpreventable) was a hegemonic vocabulary in the coverage of corporate offending.

Fourth, media coverage of Westray focused primarily on the acts of individuals rather than on the organizational context that caused and sustained the pattern of workplace death. This finding supports McCormick's (1995), Richard's (1999), Goff's (2001) and my own (McMullan and Hinze 1999, 2001) previous analyses of news coverage of Westray, as well as the larger body of media research that has found that news representations of corporate harm and death frame stories via "personalities" (Levi and Pithouse 1992; Morash and Hale 1987; Burns and Orrick 2002; Ericson et al. 1989). Cavender and Mulcahy's (1998: 706) observation that "personalizing the coverage and dwelling on notables made the stories more newsworthy" in the General Motors/NBC Dateline case was certainly true in the Westray coverage. The reporting of Westray unfolded like a "crime fiction"! Good defeated bad in the "whodunits" of policing, courtroom conflict, surprise witnesses and endless appeals. The sensationalism of this "individualization" approach provided some chilling portraits of Curragh Resources as a company and provoked severe reservations about government institutions and organizations. Although reporters depicted individuals as violators of civic boundaries, there was an absence of awe and outrage in their journalism when compared to the "vocabulary of crime" that castigated the Ford Motor Company for their role in the Pinto debacle (Randall 1987), or the insinuating reporting that normally accompanies conventional crimes like street assaults or juvenile crime. (Barak 1994, 2003; Surrette 1998).

Conversely, and unlike the reporting of the Ford Pinto deaths and injuries (Swigert and Farrell 1980), the Imperial Food Products fire (Wright et al. 1995) and the Bhopal chemical explosion (Lynch et al. 1989), a "personalization of harm" narrative was not prominent in media depictions of Westray. The press was reluctant to describe the awful deaths suffered by the victims of the explosion or to register the trauma experienced by the bereaved families. While they witnessed the grief and courage of "coping with a tragedy," their coverage did not signify the ways in which the deaths produced by the corporation were, in fact, like the homicides or manslaughters associated with conventional criminality. The newspaper reports of Westray did not transform the consciousness of the public and business community so that corporate violence could be seen as criminal in nature. As Swigert and Farrell (1980: 180) astutely observe, "before the activities of corporations can be recognized as instances of conventional crime, the social harms produced by these activities must be recognized as conventional harms."

Fifth, this retreat from a crime discourse contrasts sharply with coverage of conventional crimes, where the press draw clear relationships between victims and offenders, demarcate moral and criminal boundaries and promote social order through follow-ups and calls for penality (Surrette 1998; Chermak 1994; Barak 1994; Reiner 2002; Ericson et. al. 1989, 1991). Even though there was plurality in the coverage of Westray, official law-and-order viewpoints still monopolized the news. Press reporting of Westray did not challenge the conventional categories of "crime" and "criminality" in the public realm. As Reiner (2002: 408) notes:

> The news media reproduce order in the process of representing it... although contemporary mass communications present an appreciably open terrain for struggles for justice, the dice are loaded in favour of dominant interests — even if they have to struggle harder for their hegemony.

Despite the discursive transformation in news production after the public inquiry, the overall volume of Westray news diminished substantially over the decade. This finding corroborates Lofquist's (1997), Wright et al.'s (1995), Chermak's (1994), Barak's (1994), Ericson et al.'s (1989, 1991), Randall's (1987, 1988) and Evans and Lundman's (1983) conclusions that news coverage of judicial investigations involving corporations and their harm over-represents the preliminary phase and under-reports the later stage of legal processes; this observation reminds us that the more dominant and lasting messages may be sent and received many times over in the early reporting weeks or months. As Wright et al. (1995: 32) note in their study of the Imperial Food Products fire:

> The lack of coverage devoted to the outcome of the case — the manslaughter convictions — is also noteworthy. Again, although it was a major case of corporate violence, the criminal conviction of the company's owner either was not covered or was conveyed in a relatively short report placed deep within the pages of the newspaper.

Sixth, the coverage of Westray strived, however hesitatingly, to highlight remorse and resolution. The public inquiry did offer some closure to bereaved family members and to the public. Similar to Swigert and Farrell's (1980), Wright et al.'s (1995) and Cavender and Mulachy's (1998) findings, the press eventually tried to "officially" resolve Westray by presenting the inquiry recommendations as the "final truth" and by inscribing scandal in their story plot lines.

> What is this weasel talk that government "may have played a role in the tragedy?" The inquiry report is clear that government negligence, lassitude and incompetence did play a role in the failure to prevent a predictable disaster.... the government cannot, morally or legally, wriggle out of compensating the Westray victims' families. (*Chronicle Herald*, December 20, 1997, B11)

There were winners and losers: the miners won and Curragh Resources and the government lost! In Cavender and Mulachy's (1998: 713) words: "wrongdoing was proved or admitted," and wrongdoers were eventually punished in the press by denunciations and calls for resignations and compensation. The public inquiry functioned as a "stock-taking ceremony," but it also "wiped the slate clean" and sent the overall message that Westray was sensationally exceptional. As Bourdieu (1980) notes, part of what makes media representations "political" is the "denial of the fully social" in the circulation and consumption of symbols and images. In turn, this refusal to see the whole context creates the invisibility of what stands before us. News representations still "imagined" crime out. This was the limit of the press's ability to tell the truth to powerful corporate and state interests, the place where their truth telling was made coincident with the exercise of power. The media produced its own version of "interpretive denial": "What happened at Westray" was really "something else"! The *corporate* origins of death in the workplace was really "something else"! The violent actions reflective of economic and political interest groups was not really violence at all but something else! The loss of life was not *crime*, but "something else": "scandal," "abuse of office," "human failings," "evasion of responsibility," "corporate manipulation" or "wrongdoing." While these were critical connotations, they were terms that carried implications of political immorality rather than legal offence. They conveyed the novelty of the Westray disaster rather than the mundane character of the criminal actions leading up to the event. The press did not demarcate the corporation as capable of "killing," and the news coverage while registering a "view from below," did not reconstitute the truth of Westray as state-corporate criminality. It was as if there was an underlying "unthought element" in the news coverage that could not or would not admit the criminality of the powerful, and a "thought element" that operated to frame and maintain certain conventional sensibilities (Bourdieu 1977: 169). In the final analysis the media obscured the causes and character of the Westray disaster. As Slapper and Tombs (1999: 94) aptly remark: "where crimes are treated as scandals (or exposés, and so on)," they serve to render invisible the "normality of corporate crimes, and their locations within (and commission on behalf of) a particular organizational form — the corporation — is again obscured."

Finally, the media coverage of Westray raises the question of whether the media are now more inclined to report on white-collar and business crime. Are images of crime and law and order within the mass media reconstituting and reconfiguring the crime problem so that corporate homicide and harm no longer enjoy definitional immunity? Levi and Pithouse (1992) say yes; Wright et al. (1995) say no! One thing is certain: corporate crimes are not accurately represented as a phenomenon, or fairly represented alongside conventional crime coverage. Notwithstanding the steady coverage of events like EnRon, Walkerton, Westray, Bhopal, Challenger, Exxon, Ford and others, the overwhelming reinforcing mass of images, texts and narratives inculcate a narrow gestalt about crime. (Reiner 2002: 379–92) These messages constitute what Bennett and Ferrell (1987) call "epistemic socialization," a process where the media reflect and shape the very categories a society uses to make sense of the world and to tell itself about itself. In doing so, any focus on corporate crime has been vastly outweighed "by the steady stream… of treatments of traditional crime issues, in both 'fictional and non-fictional contexts'" (Slapper and Tombs 1999: 93). Despite the rise in investigative journalism, in advocacy groups that monitor business and the media, and in the media's own legitimacy crisis, "what exists, what matters and what happens" in regard to crime and law and order has not changed much. The more frequent reporting and condemnation of corporate harm is occurring within a general paradigm that is increasingly and cumulatively focusing on conventional crime coverage, promoting it as the "general politics of truth" about law and order. Message pluralism has not followed in the wake of media pluralism insofar as crime news is concerned. Reporters and editors, rather like corporate executives, seem to see their own virtue reflected in the guilt of those beneath them. They are not only confused about corporate crime, they are misdirected as to the distribution of crime in general. In the case of Westray, both mystification and misdirection preserved the appearance of corporate respectability and helped keep hidden to others the underlying ugly reality behind the explosion. In failing to imagine the Westray story as law-and-order news the press were not only duped by "spin doctors" (Jobb 1994: 57), they contributed to the tragic cycle of disasters that are then followed by more "public inquiries, recommendations and more disasters" (Tucker 1995: 117).

The discernible reader will detect my prescriptive message: the news media *should* have been more proactive in criminalizing the deaths of Westray and *should* have played a more critical role in exposing the truth of corporate violence, even though their occupational culture (i.e., career advancement, ratings, loyalties, promotions, etc.) and their relations to larger power structures (advertisers, owners, managers, etc.) makes that role difficult when corporate and state institutions stand accused. This is not a question of "objectively" compiling the facts, as some reporters believe. The coverage of Westray shows that the issue is not *if* the media will produce a truth reality about a deadly disaster, but rather *what* "regime of truth" will they construct. The failure of the press to criminalize the mine workers' deaths is not neutral reporting, but part of an embedded institutional discourse that misconceives and misguides the public about the enormous harms and costs that corporate violence imposes on society. Morton Mintz (1991: 9), a former reporter, put it this way: "Desensitization corrupts the news," and truth drifts away "before the winds of circumstance, timidity and self-interest."

Of course rushing to judgment must also be avoided. Exercising restraint and not prematurely portraying corporate and state officials as crass criminals is not only wise, it is legally necessary and politically sensible. Libel and public embarrassment invite costs and ridicule, which news owners, editors and reporters are concerned to avoid. But this perspective is weakened in the Westray case by two considerations mentioned earlier. First, reporters were never independent observers and recorders of the facts, but quickly developed angles for explaining the explosion — the discourse of human tragedy and the discourse of political economy. They socially produced the explosion as a non-criminal event. Second, the press were reluctant to sustain a social vocabulary of corporate crime, even when the case was being tried as a crime and afterwards, when the public inquiry was exposing the reckless, negligent and dangerous behaviour of officialdom. This disinterest may be justified on the grounds that the criminal justice system could not prove its case and eventually abandoned it. But reporters are not merely observers of public affairs, they are participants in them, and they claim to search for truth in all its complexity. Unfortunately, the deeper and more challenging questions were passed over: a search for truth, which would have exposed corporate violence and taught us wisely about this shocking event, was blunted by news narratives that reduced explanation and understanding to the emotion of the moment or the bankruptcy of the political. Westray was reported as the crime that never happened!

Criminologists, for their part, are not exempt from the responsibility to tell the truth of corporate crime. They too have priorized the study of sensational, conventional crimes and victims, and downplayed the study of media representations of corporate misconduct (Surrette 1998; Barak 2003). While much of this research has exposed media distortions of crime and the criminal justice system, criminologists also need to challenge the media to reflect upon their news making and join the public debate about the seriousness and changing public conceptions of corporate violence. Barak (1994: 6, 12) sums up this challenge well: news-making criminologists should insist that the media "'tell it like it is,' and better yet, 'like it could be' or 'like it should be.'" In studying the media, they "should interject their own characterizations and images of crime and justice for the purpose of redefining these social stories." They should recover, restore and validate the underemphasized and unspoken discourses that dare to call a crime by its name! My hope is that this small book goes some way to meeting that large challenge.

# References

Adorno, T.W. 1991. *The Culture of Industry: Selected Essays on Mass Culture*. London: Routledge.

Arendt, H. 1971. *Between Past and Future: Eight Exercises in Political Thought*. New York: Viking.

_____. 1972. *The Crises of the Republic*. New York: Harcourt Brace Jovanovich.

Arendt, T.W. 1995. *Eichmann in Jerusalem: A Report on the Banality of Evil*. New York: Penguin.

Awad, J. 1985. *The Power of Public Relations*. New York: Paeger.

Banks, M. 2001. *Visual Methods in Social Research*. Thousand Oaks, CA: Sage.

Barak, G. (ed.). 1997. *Representing O.J.: Murder, Criminal Justice and Mass Culture*. Albany, New York: Harrow and Heston.

_____. 1994. "Media, Society and Criminology." In G. Barak (ed.), *Media, Process, and the Social Construction of Crime: Studies in Newsmaking Criminology*. New York: Garland Publishing.

_____. 2003 "Mediated Value: Production, Distortion and Consumption." Paper presented at Criminal Media Conference, Saint Thomas University, Fredericton, NB, October.

Barlow, M.H., D.E. Barlow and T.G. Chiricos. 1995. "Economic Conditions and Ideologies of Crime in the Media: A Content Analysis of Crime News." *Crime and Delinquency* 41(1): 3–19.

Becker, H. 1963. *Outsiders: Studies in the Sociology of Deviance*. New York: The Free Press.

_____. 1967. "Whose Side Are We On?" *Social Problems* 14, 239–47.

Bennett, S., and J. Ferrell. 1987. "Music Videos and Epistemic Socialization." *Youth and Society* 18(3): 44–62.

Berry, J. 1992. *Lead Us Not into Temptation: Catholic Priests and the Sexual Abuse of Children*. Toronto: Doubleday.

Beveridge, D.R., and P.J. Duncan. 2000. *Review of the Nova Scotia Public Prosecution Service: Report on the Westray Prosecution*. Halifax: NS Department of Justice.

Bohm, R.M. 1994. "Social Relationships that Arguably Should Be Criminal Although They Are Not: On the Political Economy of Crime." In G. Barak (ed.), *Media, Process, and the Social Construction of Crime: Studies in Newsmaking Criminology*. New York: Garland Publishing.

Bourdieu, P. 1977. *Outline of a Theory of Practice*. Cambridge: Cambridge University Press.

_____. 1980. "The Production of Belief." *Media, Culture and Society* 2(3).

Boyd, Susan C., D. Chunn and R. Menzies. 2001. *(Ab)using power*. Halifax: Fernwood.

Brown, S. 2003. *Crime and Law in Media Culture*. Philadelphia: Open University Press.

Burns, R.G., and L. Orrick. 2002. "Assessing Newspaper Coverage of Corporate Violence: The Dance Hall Fire in Goteborg, Sweden." *Critical Criminology* 11: 137–50.

Calvitta, Kance, and N. Portell. 1994. "The State and White Collar Crime: Saving the Savings and Loans." *Law and Society Review* 28: 297–324.

Cameron, S., and A. Mitorvica. 1994. "Burying Westray." *Saturday Night* 109, 4 May.

Canada. Supreme Court. 1994. United Steel Workers of America, Local 9332 and the Honourable Justice KI. *Peter Richard and Gerald Phillips, Roger Parry, Glynn Jones, Arnold Smith, Robert Parry, Brian Palmer and Kevin Atherton, and the Attorney General of Nova Scotia and Westray Families' Group and Town of Stellarton*. Ottawa: Supreme Court of Canada.

Carlen, P. 2004. "Official discourse, comic relief and the play of governance." In G. Gilligan and J.Pratt (eds.), *Crime, Truth and Justice: Official Inquiry Discourse, Knowledge*. Cullompton, UK: Willan

Cavender, G., and A. Mulcahy. 1998. "Trial by Fire: Media Constructions of Corporate Deviance." *Justice Quarterly* 15(4): 697–717.

Chermak, S. 1994. "Crime in the News Media: A Refined Understanding of How Crimes Become News." In G. Barak (ed.), *Media, Process, and the Social Construction of Crime: Studies in Newsmaking Criminology*. New York: Garland Publishing.

_____. 1995. *Victims in the News: Crime in American News Media*. Boulder: Westview.

Chibnall, S. 1977. *Law and Order News*. London: Tavistock.

Coffey, A., and P. Atkinson. 1996. *Making Sense of Qualitative Data: Complimentary Research Designs*. Thousand Oaks: Sage.

Cohen, S. 1993. "Human Rights and Crimes of the State: The Culture of Denial." *Australian and New Zealand Journal of Criminology* 26: 97–115.

_____. 1996. "Government Responses to Human Rights Reports: Claims, Denials and Counterclaims." *Human Rights Quarterly* 18: 517–43.

_____. 2001. *States of Denial: Knowing About Atrocities and Suffering*. Cambridge: Polity.

Comish, S. 1993. *The Westray Tragedy: A Miner's Story*. Halifax: Fernwood.

Comish, S., and S. Comish. 1999. "The Road to Recovery is Long." In C. McCormick (ed.), *The Westray Chronicles: A Case Study in Corporate Crime*. Halifax: Fernwood.

Counihan, T.M. 1975. "Reading Television: Notes on the Problems of Media Content." *Australian and New Zealand Journal of Sociology* 11(2): 31–36.

Croall, H. 1992. *White Collar Crime*. Buckingham: Open University Press.

Cullen, F.T., W.J. Maskestad and G. Cavender. 1987. *Corporate Crime Under Attack: The Ford Pinto Case and Beyond*. Cincinnati: Anderson.

Davis, C.G. 2003. "Picking up the Pieces: The Personal Legacies of Westray." Paper presented at the Congress of the Humanities and Social Sciences, June 1, Halifax, Nova Scotia.

Dean, M. 1994. *Critical and Effective Histories: Foucault's Methods and Historical Sociology*. New York: Routledge.

Dodd, S. 1999. "Unsettled Accounts after Westray." In C. McCormick (ed.), *The Westray Chronicles: A Case Study in Corporate Crime*. Halifax: Fernwood.

Dominick, J. 1978. "Crime and Law Enforcement in the Mass Media." In C. Winick (ed.), *Deviance and the Mass Media*. Beverly Hills, CA: Sage.

Eco, U. 1979. *The Role of the Reader*. London: Hutchison.

Ericson, R., P. Baranek, and J. Chan. 1987. *Visualizing Deviance*. Toronto: University of Toronto Press.

_____. 1989. *Negotiating Control: A Study of News Sources*. Toronto: University of Toronto Press.

_____. 1991. *Representing Order: Crime, Law and Justice in the News Media*. Toronto: University of Toronto Press.

Ermann, M.D., and R.J. Lundman. 1996. *Corporate and Governmental Deviance*. Fifth edition. New York: Oxford.

Evans, S.S., and R.J. Lundman. 1983. "Newspaper Coverage of Corporate Price-Fixing." *Criminology* 21(4): 529–41.

Evans, T.D., F.T. Cullen, and P.J. Dubeck. 1993. "Public Perceptions of Corporate Crime." In M.B. Blankenship (ed.), *Understanding Corporate Criminality*. New York: Garland.

Ewick, P., and S.S. Silbey. 1995. "Toward a Sociology of Narrative." *Law and Society Review* 29(2): 197–226.

Fishman, M. 1980. *Manufacturing the News*. Austin: University of Texas Press.

Fiske, J. 1987. *Television Culture*. New York: Rouledge.

Fleras, A., and J. Lock Kunz. 2001. *Media and Minorities: Representing Diversity in a Multicultural Canada*. Toronto: Thompson Educational Publishing.

Foucault, M. 1977 "Nietzsche, Genealogy, History." In D.F. Bouchard (ed.), *Language, Counter-Memory, Practice: Selected Essays and Interviews by Michel Foucault*. Blackwell, Oxford.

_____. 1980a. "Truth and Power." In C. Gordon (ed.).

_____. 1980b. "Two Lectures." In C. Gordon (ed.).

_____. 1980c. "Power and Strategies." In C. Gordon (ed.).

_____. 1980d. The Eye of Power. In C. Gordon (ed.).

_____. 1980e. "The History of Sexuality." In C. Gordon (ed.).

_____. 1981. "The Order of Discourse." In R. Young (ed.), *Untying the Text: A Post-Structuralist Reader*. London: Routledge.

_____. 1982. "Power and Truth." In H.L. Dreyfus and P. Rabinow (eds.), Michel Foucault: Beyond Structuralism and Hermeneutics. Second edition. Chicago: University of Chicago Press.

_____. 1988a. *The Archaeology of Knowledge and the Discourse on Language: Michel Foucault*. New York: Harper Colophon.

_____. 1988b. "The Concern for Truth." In L.D. Kritzman (ed.), *Politics, Philosophy, Culture: Interviews and Other Writings of Michel Foucault, 1977–1984*. New York: Routledge, Chapman and Hall.

_____. 1989. "The Concern for Truth." In S. Lotringer (ed.), *Foucault Live: Interviews (1966–84), Michel Foucault*. New York: Semiotext(e) Foreign Agents Series.

_____. 1990. *The History of Sexuality*. New York: Vintage.

_____. 1991a. "The Discourse on Power." In R.J. Goldstein and J. Cascaito (trans.), *Michel Foucault: Remarks on Marx. Conversations with Duccio Trombadori*. New York: Semiotext(e).

_____. 1991b. "Politics and the Study of Discourse." In G. Burchell, C. Gordon and P. Miller (eds.), *The Foucault Effect: Studies in Governmentality*. Chicago: University of Chicago Press.

_____. 1991c. "Questions of Method." In G. Burchell, C. Gordon, and P. Miller (eds.), *The Foucault Effect: Studies in Governmentality*. Chicago: University of Chicago Press.

_____. 1995. *Discipline and Punish: The Birth of the Prison*. New York: Vintage.

_____. 1998. "Power and Sex." In L.D. Kritzman (ed.), *Michel Foucault: Politics, Philosophy and Culture*. New York: Routledge.

_____. 1999. "Is It Useless to Revolt?" In J.M. Carrette (ed.), *Religion and Culture: Michel Foucault*. New York: Routledge.

_____. 2001. *Fearless Speech*. Los Angeles: Semiotexte.

_____. 2003. *Society Must be Defended: Lectures at the College of France, 1975–1976*. New York: Picador.

Frank, M. 1989. "On Foucault's Concept of Discourse." In T. Armstrong (ed.), *Michel Foucault: Philosopher*. New York: Routledge.

Friedrichs, D. 1996. *White Collar Crime: Trusted Criminals in Contemporary Society*. Belmont, CA: Wadsworth.

Gamson, W.A., D. Croteau, W. Hoynes, and T. Sasson. 1992. "Media Images and the Social Construction of Reality." *Annual Reviews in Sociology* 18: 373–93.

Gamson, W.A., and A. Modigliani. 1989. "Media Discourse and Public Opinion on Nuclear Power." *American Journal of Sociology* 95: 1–37.

Gans, H.J. 1980. *Deciding What's News: A Study of CBS Evening News, NBC Nightly News, Newsweek and Time*. New York: Vintage.

Gilligan, G. 2004. "Official Inquiry, Truth and Criminal Justice." In G. Gilligan and J.Pratt (eds.), *Crime, Truth and Justice: Official Inquiry, Discourse, Knowledge*. Cullompton, UK: Willan.

Gilligan, G., and J. Pratt. 2004. "Introduction: Crime, Truth and Justice — Official Inquiry and the Production of Knowledge." In G. Gilligan and J. Pratt (eds.), *Crime, Truth and Justice: Official Inquiry, Discourse, Knowledge*. Cullompton, UK: Willan.

Gitlin, T. 1980. *The Whole World is Watching*. Berkely: Univeristy of California Press.

Glasbeek, H. 2003. *Wealth by Stealth: Corporate Crime, Corporate Law and the Perversion of Democracy*. Toronto: Between The Lines.

Glasbeek, H., and E. Tucker. 1999. "Death by Consensus at Westray?" In C. McCormick (ed.), *The Westray Chronicles: A Case Study in Corporate Crime*. Halifax, Fernwood.

Goff, C. 2001. "The Westray Mine Disaster: Media Coverage of a Corporate Crime in Canada." In H.N. Pontell and D. Shichor (eds.), *Contemporary Issues in Crime and Criminal Justice: Essays in Honor of Gilbert Geis*. Upper Saddle River, NJ: Prentice-Hall.

Gordon, C. (ed.). 1980. *Power/Knowledge: Selected Interviews and Other Writings (1972–1977), Michel Foucault*. New York: Pantheon.

Hancock, N., and A. Liebling. 2004. "Truth, Independence and Effectiveness in Prison Inquiries." In G. Gilligan and J. Pratt (eds.), *Crime, Truth and Justice: Official Inquiry: Discourse, Knowledge*. Cullompton, UK: Willan.

Hall, S., J. Jefferson, and B. Roberts. 1978. *Policing the Crisis*. London: Macmillan.

Harris, M. 1990. *Unholy Orders: Tragedy at Mount Cashel*. Markham, ON: Penguin.

Herman, E.S., and N. Chomsky. 1989. *Manufacturing Consent: The Political Economy of the Mass Media*. New York: Pantheon Books.

Hynes, T., and P. Prasad. 1999. "The Normal Violation of Safety Rules." In C. McCormick (ed.), *The Westray Chronicles: A Case Study in Corporate Crime*. Halifax: Fernwood.

Iyengar, S. 1991. *Is Anyone Responsible?: How Television News Frame Political Issues*. Chicago: University of Chicago Press.

Jobb, D. 1994. *Calculated Risk: Greed, Politics and the Westray Tragedy*. Halifax: Nimbus.

_____. 1999. "Legal Disaster: Westray and the Justice System." In C. McCormick (ed.), *The Westray Chronicles: A Case Study in Corporate Crime*. Halifax: Fernwood.

Jones, R.A. 1996. *Research Methods in the Social and Behavioral Sciences*. Second edition. Sunderland, MA: Sinauer Associates.

Kappeler, V., M. Blumberg, and G. Potter. 2000. *The Mythology of Crime and Criminal Justice*. Third edition. Prospect Heights, IL: Waveland.

Kellner, D. 1990. *Television and the Crisis of Democracy*. Boulder: Westview.

Kendall, G., and G. Wickham. 1999. *Using Foucault's Methods*. London: Sage.

Knight, S. 1980. *Form and Ideology in Crime Fiction*. Bloomington: Indiana University Press.

Lea, J. 2004. "From Brixton to Bradford: Official Discourse on Race and Urban Violence in the United Kingdom." In G. Gillian and J. Pratt (eds.), *Crime, Truth and Justice: Official Inquiry, Discourse, Knowledge*. Cullompton, UK: Willan.

Leman-Langlois, S., and C.D. Shearing. 2004. "Repairing the Future: the South African Truth and Reconciliation Commission at Work." In G. Gilligan and J. Pratt (eds.), *Crime, Truth and Justice: Official Inquiry, Discourse, Knowledge*. Cullompton, UK: Willan.

Lester, M. 1980. "Generating Newsworthiness: The Interpretative Construction of Public Events." *American Sociological Review* 45: 984–94.

Levi, M. 1987. *Regulating Fraud: White Collar Crime and the Criminal Process*. London: Tavistock.

Levi, M., and A. Pithouse. 1992. "The Victims of Fraud." In D. Downes (ed.), *Unravelling Criminal Justice*. London: Macmillan.

Liberal Party of Canada. 1992. *Westray Mine Disaster: Documents of the Liberal Opposition*. Ottawa: Liberal Party of Canada.

Liska, A., and W. Baccaglini. 1990. "Feeling Safe by Comparison: Crime in the Newspapers." *Social Problems* 37: 360–74.

Lofquist, W.S. 1997. "Constructing 'Crime': Media Coverage of Individual and Organizational Wrongdoing." *Justice Quarterly* 14(2): 243–63.

Lynch, M.J., M.K. Nalla, and K.W. Miller. 1989. "Cross-Cultural Perceptions of Deviance: The Case of Bhopal." *Journal of Research in Crime and Delinquency* 26(1): 7–35.

Lynch, M.J., P. Stretesky, and P. Hammond. 2000. "Media Coverage of Chemical Crimes, Hillsborough County, Florida, 1987–97." *British Journal of Criminology* 27(2): 16–29.

Manning, P.K., and B. Cullum-Swan. 1994. "Narrative, Context and Semiotic Analysis." In N.K. Densin and Y.S. Lincoln (eds.), *Handbook of Qualitative Research*. Thousand Oaks: Sage.

Maxfield, M.G., and E. Babbie. 2001. *Research Methods for Criminal Justice and Criminology*. Belmont, CA: Woodsworth.

McCormick, C. 1995. "The Westray Mine Explosion: Covering a Disaster and a Failed Inquiry." In C. McCormick (ed.), *Constructing Danger: The Mis/Representation of Crime in the News*. Halifax: Fernwood.

_____. 1999. *The Westray Chronicles*. Halifax: Fernwood.

McMullan, J. 1992. *Beyond the Limits of the Law: Corporate Crime and Law and Order*. Halifax: Fernwood.

_____. 2001. "Westray and After: Power, Truth and News Reporting of the Westray

Mine Disaster." In S.C. Boyd, D.E. Chunn and R. Menzies (eds.), *[Ab]using Power: The Canadian Experience*. Halifax: Fernwood.

McMullan, J., and S. Hinze. 1999. "The Press, Ideology, and Corporate Crime." In C. McCormick (ed.), *The Westray Chronicles: A Case Study in Corporate Crime*. Halifax: Fernwood.

McMullan J., and M. McClung. 2003. "Crime Out: Press Reporting, News, Truth and the Westray Public Inquiry." Media and Crime Conference, Fredericton, NB, October.

_____. 2005. "The Media, the Politics of Truth, and the Coverage of Corporate Violence: The Westray disaster and the public inquiry." Forthcoming.

McQuail, D. 1992. *Media Performance: News Communication and the Public Interest*. London: Sage

Mintz, M. 1991. "Media Coverups of Corporate Crime." *Propaganda Review* 9: 18–21; 62–63.

Moeller, S. 1999. *Compassion Fatigue: How the Media Sell Disease, Famine, War and Death*. New York: Routledge.

Molotch, H., and M. Lester. 1978. "Accidental News: The Great Oil Spill as Local Occurrence and National Event." In M.D. Ermann and R.J. Lundman (eds.), *Corporate and Governmental Deviance: Problems of Organizational Behavior in Contemporary Society*. New York: Oxford University Press.

Morash, M., and D. Hale. 1987. "Unusual Crime or Crime as Unusual? Images of Corruption in the Interstate Commerce Commission." In T.S. Bynum (ed.), *Organized Crime in America: Concepts and Controversies*. New York: Oxford University Press.

Murdock, G. 1982. "Disorderly Images." In C.S. Sumner (ed.), *Crime, Justice and the Mass Media*. Cambridge: Cambridge University Institute of Criminology.

Neuman, L.W. 2003. *Social Research Methods: Qualitative and Quantitative Approaches*. Fifth edition. New York: Allyn and Bacon.

Nova Scotia Department of Labour. 1992. *Westray Disaster: Ministerial Statements to the Press and House of Assembly/by Leroy Legere*. Halifax.

Paletz, D., and R. Entman. 1981. *Media, Power, Politics*. New York: Free Press.

Potter, G.W., and V.E. Kappeller (eds.). 1998. *Constructing Crime: Perspectives on Making News and Social Problems*. Prospect Heights: Waveland.

Province of Nova Scotia. 1989. *Coal Mines Regulation Act*. Halifax.

_____. 1992. *Debates of the House of Assembly*. Transcript. May 15: 9392-93.

_____. 1995. *Workers' Compensation Act*. Halifax.

_____. 1996. *Occupational Health and Safety Act*. Halifax.

_____. 1997. *Public Inquiry Transcripts*. Vol. 67: 14440.

Randall, D. 1987. "The Portrayal of Business Malfeasance in the Elite and General Public Media." *Social Science Quarterly* 68.

_____. 1995. "The Portrayal of Business Malfeasance in the Elite and General Media." In G. Geis, R.F. Meier and L.M. Salinger (eds.), *White-Collar Crime: Classic and Contemporary Views*. Third edition. Toronto: Free Press.

Randall, D.M., L. Lee-Sammons, and P.R. Hagner. 1988. "Common Versus Elite Crime Coverage in Network News." *Social Science Quarterly* 69: 919–29.

Reiner, R. 2002. "Media Made Criminology: The Representation of Crime in the Mass Media." In M. Maguire, R. Morgan and R. Reiner (eds.), *The Oxford Handbook of Criminology*. London: Oxford Press.

Richard, P. 1997. *The Westray Story: A Predictable Path to Disaster: Report of the*

*Westray Mine Public Inquiry*. Halifax: Westray Mine Public Inquiry.

Richards, T. 1999. "Public Relations and the Westray Mine Explosion." In C. McCormick (ed.), The Westray Chronicles: A Case Study in Corporate Crime. Halifax: Fernwood.

Ricoeur, P. 1980: "Narrative Time." In W.J. Thomas (ed.), *On Narrative*. Chicago: University of Chicago Press.

Riffe, D., and Freitag, A. 1997. "A Content Analysis of Content Analysis: Twenty-Five Years of Journalism Quarterly." *Journalism and Mass Communications Quarterly* 3: 515–24.

Roberts, A., and A. Doob. 1990. "News Media Influences on Sentencing." *Law and Human Behavior* 14(5): 451–68.

Rock, P. 1973. "News as Eternal Recurrance." In S. Cohen and J. Young (eds.), *The Manufacture of News*. London: Constable.

Rothberg, R.I., and D. Thompson (eds.). 2000. *Truth vs. Justice: The Morality of Truth Commissions*. Princeton: Princeton University Press.

Rouse, J. 1994. "Power/Knowledge." In G. Gutting (ed.), *The Cambridge Companion to Foucault*. Cambridge: Cambridge University Press.

Sacco, V. 1995. "Media Constructions of Crime." *The Annals of the American Academy of Political and Social Sciences* 539: 141–54.

Scheper-Hughes, N. 1998. "Institutionalized Sex Abuse and the Catholic Church." In N. Scheper-Hughes and C. Sargent (eds.), *Small Wars: The Cultural Politics of Childhood*. Berkeley: University of California Press.

Schiller, D. 1986. "Transformations of News in the U.S. Information Market." In P. Golding et al. (eds.), *Communicating Politics*. New York: Holms and Meier.

Scott, M.B., and S.M. Lyman. 1970. "Accounts, Deviance, and Social Order." In J.D. Douglas (ed.), *Deviance and Respectability: The Social Construction of Moral Meaning*. New York: Basic Books.

Scraton, P. 1999. *Hillsborough: The Truth*. Edinburgh: Mainstream.

_____. 2004. "From Deceit to Disclosure: The Politics of Official Inquiries in the United Kingdom." In G. Gilligan and J. Pratt (eds.), *Crime, Truth and Justice: Official Inquiry, Discourse, Knowledge*. Cullompton, UK: Willan.

Scraton, P., A. Jemphrey, and S. Coleman. 1995. *No Last Rights: The Denial of Justice and the Promotion of Myth in the Aftermath of the Hillsborough Disaster*. Liverpool: CC Alden.

Slapper, G., and S. Tombs. 1999. *Corporate Crime*. London: Longman.

Smith, C. 1992. *Media and the Apocalypse: News Coverage of the Yellowstone Forest Fires, Exxon Valdez Oil Spill, and Loma Prieta Earthquake*. Westport: Greenwood Press.

Smith, D. N.d. *Westray Incident Report*. Prepared for the Emergency Measures Organization, unpublished.

Snider, L. 1993. *Bad Business: Corporate Crime in Canada*. Scarborough: Nelson Canada.

Sturken, M., and L. Cartwright. 2001. *Practices of Looking: An Introduction to Visual Culture*. New York: Oxford University Press.

Sumner, C.S., and S. Sandberg. 1990. "The Press Censure of 'Dissident Minorities': The Ideology of Parlimentary Democracy, Thatcherism and Policing the Crisis." In C.S. Sumner (ed.), *Censure, Politics and Criminal Justice*. Milton Keynes: Open University Press.

Surrette, R. 1998. *Media, Crime and Criminal Justice: Images and Realities*. Belmont:

CA: West/Wadsworth.

Swigert, V.L., and R.A. Farrell. 1980. "Corporate Homicide: Definitional Processes in the Creation of Deviance." *Law and Society Review* 15: 161–82.

Sykes, G., and D. Matza. 1998. "Techniques of Neutralization: A Theory of Delinquency." In F.P. Williams and M. McShane (eds.), *Criminological Theory: Selected Classic Readings*. Cincinnati: Anderson.

Tombs, S., and D. Whyte. 2001. "Reporting Corporate Crime Out of Existence." *Criminal Justice Matters* 43: 22–23.

Tucker, E. 1995. "The Westray Mine Disaster and Its Aftermath: The Politics of Causation." *CJLS/RCDS* 10(1): 92–123.

Tumber, H. 1993. "Selling Scandal: Business and the Media." *Media Culture and Society* 15: 345–61.

Tunnell, K. 1998. "Reflections on Crime, Criminals, and Control in News Magazine and Television Programs." In F. Bailey and D. Hale (eds.), *Popular Culture, Crime and Justice*. Belmont: West/Wadsworth.

van Dijk, T.A. 1991. *Racism and the Press*. New York: Routledge.

_____. 1993. "Principles of Critical Discourse Analysis." *Discourse and Society* 4(2): 249–83.

_____. 1998. "Opinion and Ideologies in the Press." In A Bell and P. Garrett (eds.), *Approaches to Media Discourse*. Oxford: Blackwell.

Walters, L., L. Wilkins, and T. Waters. 1989. *Bad Tidings: Communications and Catastrophe*. Hillsdale, NJ: Laurence Erlbaum.

Welch, M., M. Fenwich, and M. Roberts. 1998. "State Managers, Intellectuals and the Media: A Content Analysis of Ideology in Experts' Quotes in Feature Newspaper articles on Crime." *Justice Quarterly* 15.

Westray Response Committee (N.S.). 1997. *Westray: A Plan of Action: Government's Response to the Report of the Westray Mine Public Inquiry*. Halifax: Westray Response Committee.

Wilde, G.J.S. 1999. "The Awareness and Acceptance of Risk at Westray." In C. McCormick (ed.), *The Westray Chronicles: A Case Study in Corporate Crime*. Halifax: Fernwood.

Williams, B. 2002. *Truth and Truthfulness: An Essay in Genealogy*. Princeton: Princeton University Press.

Williams, R. 1989. *What I Came to Say*. London: Hutchison.

Wright, J.P., F.T. Cullen, and M.B. Blankenship. 1995. "The Social Construction of Corporate Violence: Media Coverage of the Imperial Food Products Fire." *Crime and Delinquency* 41(1): 20–36.

Wykes, M. 2001. *News, Crime and Culture*. London: Pluto.